500 DAYS

(TRANSITION TO THE MARKET)

G. Yavlinsky, B. Fedorov, S. Shatalin,
N. Petrakov, S. Aleksashenko, A. Vavilov,
L. Grigoriev, M. Zadornov, V. Machits,
A. Mikhailov, E. Yasin

**A Working Group formed by a joint decision of
M. S. Gorbachev and B. N. Yeltsin**

The Concept and Program of *500 DAYS (Transition to the Market)* were drawn up between August 2 and 31 by a working group composed of the following:

S. Shatalin
N. Petrakov
G. Yavlinsky
S. Aleksashenko
A. Vavilov
L. Grigoriev
M. Zadornov
V. Machits
A. Mikhailov
B. Fedorov
E. Yasin

Also taking part in the group's deliberations were V. Martynov and T. Yarygina.

500 DAYS

(TRANSITION TO THE MARKET)

G. Yavlinsky, B. Fedorov, S. Shatalin,
N. Petrakov, S. Aleksashenko, A. Vavilov,
L. Grigoriev, M. Zadornov, V. Machits,
A. Mikhailov, E. Yasin

English translation edited by David Kushner

St. Martin's Press
New York

Transition to the Market: the Concept and Program *was first printed in Russian on September 5, 1990. The Cultural Initiative and the Soros Foundation—Soviet Union have provided this translation to the authors as a courtesy.*

The English translation was edited by David S. Kushner.

English translation © St. Martin's Press, 1991

First Published in the United States of America in 1991

Printed in the United States of America

ISBN 0-312-07396-8

Library of Congress Cataloging-in-Publication Data

500 days : transition to the market / G. Yavlinski . . . [et al.] :
    English translation edited by David Kushner.
        p.   cm.
    Translated from Russian.
    Includes index.
    ISBN 0-312-07396-8
    1. Soviet Union—Economic policy—1986– 2. Perestroika.
  I. Yavlinsky, G. (Grigori)   II. Kushner, David S.   III. Title: Five
  hundred days.
HC336.26.A17   1991
338.947'009'049—dc20   91-31134
                                                                    CIP

CONTENTS

Man, Freedom, and Market

PART I
The concept of the program for transition to a market economy as the foundation for an Economic Union of sovereign republics

PART II
The Basic Blocks of the Transition Program

PART III
Structural Policy and Conversion

PART IV
Legislative and Organizational
Support for Economic Reform

PART V
Supplement

MAN, FREEDOM, AND MARKET

On the Program Developed by the Task Force Headed by Academician S. S. Shatalin

This program could happen only in the era of perestroika which began in 1985. It is a natural outgrowth of that policy. M. S. Gorbachev and B. N. Yeltsin initiated the program and it can be realized only if they unite their efforts in its support.

The long rule of the totalitarian sociopolitical system dragged our society into a profound crisis. Indecisiveness of the government and the mistakes it made in economic policy brought the country to the brink of collapse. Life is getting more and more difficult, and people are becoming desperate. Only well-calculated and energetic actions, supported by the people, and relying upon their unity and patriotism, can achieve a breakthrough.

Our society has developed an extreme experience of economic reforms, which people have come to associate only with changes for the worse in their lives. Life, unfortunately, has taught them to believe more easily in bad than in good things. The realization of the suggested program is expected to combat this sentiment.

Its basic difference from all previous attempts lies in the fact that it relies upon a fundamentally new economic concept. It plans to move toward a market-oriented economy at the expense of the state, but not at the expense of the people.

For a long time, economic policy did not consider the people's interests. The state was wealthy while the people were poor. The state accumulated under its control almost all the resources for production. Such resources were thoughtlessly squandered on giant and ineffective projects, for increasing military power, and for certain ideologically flavored practices overseas, even though the time has long passed since we could afford this.

This program sets forth the task of taking everything possible from the state and giving it over to the people. There are good reasons to believe that giving back to the people a considerable part of property and resources on various terms will ensure more effective use of these resources and forestall many negative side effects in the transition to a market economy. It is necessary to slash dramatically all state expenditures, including those kept secret from the people.

Only when the people see that all the possibilities and resources currently devoured by the giant state machine have been channeled to serve the people will the leadership of the country be in a position to appeal to the people to be patient, to take up another heavy load in the name of the motherland and of their own future and the future of their children.

We must also turn to other countries for assistance. They will support us if they consider our program decisive and efficient and if they are convinced that the assistance they grant will find a reasonable and effective use for the good of the people.

Each person, each enterprise, each area or sovereign republic is sure to find in the suggested program a response to its own individual interests and a chance to start immediately realizing those interests.

Another basic feature of the program is that people should not wait for permission or orders, but should act in their own best interests. The program shows how to do it in the best and most effective way. Anybody who carefully reads this program can decide what is good for him and make a preliminary estimate of what he should do and what terms he should demand for the realization of his economic rights and interests.

Nobody seeks to impose anything on anybody. Everybody has a right to choose, guided by his own wishes and capabilities, whether to become an entrepreneur, an employee of the state apparatus, or a manager at a stock company, to engage in individual labor, or to become a member of a co-op. The reform grants citizens the right to economic self-determination, setting the rules which will prevent certain people, groups, enterprises, and regions from infringing upon the economic rights of others while pursuing their own interests. It is freedom of choice which is the basis for personal freedom and for the realization of individual creative potential. These are not yet rules for the future market economy, which will emerge only in the course of the formation and development of a market-oriented society. The economic thrust of the suggested program is the transition to the market, laying the groundwork for a society based upon new economic principles.

It is the system of economic relations and management of the economic complex created in this country that is to blame for the fact that a very hard-working people in a very rich country live at a standard which in no way matches the resources of the territory or the people's talents and effort. People live much worse than they work, because either they make things they do not need or what they make is being lost or misused.

The suggested program develops ways of transition to an economic system which could transform this situation and grant to every citizen a real opportunity to make his or her life better. Thus the program can be considered as a guide to realizing the right of citizens to a better, more decent life.

THE RIGHT TO PROPERTY

The right to property is realized through denationalization and privatization, giving over state property to citizens. By giving property back to the people, the social orientation of the economy will manifest itself. This is not an act of revenge, but an act of social justice, a way to fix the right of man to his share of the present and future national wealth. Privatization, it should be emphasized, is also a way to distribute responsibility for the state and the level of development of the society to all citizens who choose to accept such responsibility. Privatization should be absolutely voluntary; it should in no way remind one of collectivization.

Property in the hands of everyone is a guarantee of stability in society and one of the important conditions to prevent social and national disasters. A person who has his own house and a plot of land, which he can at any time give over to his children, a person who owns shares or other securities, is objectively interested in the stability of society, in social and national peace and harmony. And, on the contrary, our sad experience shows how dangerous for the society, for its normal functioning and development, is a person who has nothing to lose.

The program gives equal chances to everybody. But this equality of opportunity should not be seen as a mirror reflection of egalitarianism. To prevent privatization from becoming a means of legal and inordinate enrichment of the few, the procedure must ensure mass participation in ownership relations; practically everybody, even if he does not have any considerable initial capital, will have an opportunity to get his share of the national wealth. Equality of opportunity will be provided by a variety of forms of privatization which will give a chance either to lease property, buy it on credit, or acquire it on a shareholding basis.

Fundamentally important is the fact that the state cannot and should not give away its property without compensation. Property must be earned, because people do not believe in free property and do not value it sufficiently.

But at the same time a part of state property should be considered already earned by people, and it can be given to them free or at a symbolic price; for example, small apartments in which people have lived for a long time, small weekend farms, and so on.

Immediately after that we must start working to establish 50 to 60 stock companies out of big state enterprises by the end of the year, and also to give over or sell at a symbolic price certain (actually already earned) categories of housing and plots of land.

An inventory of the national riches of the country should be made, primarily of gold and currency reserves, strategic reserves, property of public organizations, unfinished construction, armed forces property, and some other types of state property (cars, state dachas, and so on.). Local soviets (district and city) will make inventories of uninhabited properties and freeze the major part of industrial construction projects upon inventory of the unfinished construction. The value of such property, of equipment not yet in place, of material resources in construction, will be estimated. Having done all this work, it will be possible to start selling enterprises, cooperatives, and a part of material resources to the public.

Local soviets will estimate the price of trade enterprises, consumer services, local industries, small- and medium-sized enterprises of other industries. After the analysis of their financial position, the local press will publish lists of these enterprises with the dates and terms of their privatization. Then, under conditions of absolute glasnost regarding the course of privatization, they will start selling uninhabited space, small enterprises, workshops, stores, stands. The program is aimed at giving people the opportunity to spend their money to buy property. Channeling a considerable amount of demand in this direction will help avoid rampant inflation as price controls are abolished by stages.

Local soviets will also make inventories of agricultural land, taking into consideration how it is being used. These actions will provide access to land to everybody who wants to farm. At the same time there will be more land sold to people for weekend farming. Smaller plots will be sold at moderate prices; larger plots, at normal market prices.

Special privatization bodies and land reform committees, along with regional and district soviets, will bear the main responsibility for realizing the citizenry's right to own property.

The right of private economic activity is provided by the redistribution of property between the state and citizens in the course of denationalization, and also by the adoption of the law on entrepreneurship. The state will create an economic environment conducive to initiative and enterprise, will make the procedure of starting one's own business easier, and will support small businesses over big enterprises via reduced taxes and favorable credits. The program is built on the assumption that society needs small enterprises to orient production to the needs of every person, to fight the dictatorship of monopolies in consumer and production markets, and to create a favorable environment for quick introduction of new scientific and technological ideas (which are best accepted by small- and medium-sized enterprises).

THE RIGHT OF CITIZENS TO ECONOMIC ACTIVITY

But how will the people's right to property actually be realized?

On the very first day of the program, equality of rights for any physical and juridical person to engage in economic activity will be declared. There will come an announcement of the privatization program, changing big industrial enterprises into stock companies and selling off small trade, public catering, and consumer services enterprises. The same statement will announce property rights guarantees for any kind of property except property belonging exclusively to the state. Amnesty for those convicted of entrepreneurship will be announced, and the entrepreneurship articles will be removed from the Criminal and Administrative Codes. Simultaneously, the struggle against the prohibitions on private property will be intensified.

The law will guarantee favorable conditions to denationalize enterprises on the initiative of work collectives. They are supposed to apply to the state property fund and the republics' state property management committees.

The state will stimulate the development of international economic contacts and encourage trips abroad to work and study. Attempts to build a system screened from the outside world have resulted in the degradation and stagnation of most of our industries. Opening up the domestic market will force our entrepreneurs to compete with cheap imported goods. This will make our economy dynamic and flexible in catering to the market and, through the market, to the consumer.

THE RIGHT OF CITIZENS TO FREEDOM OF THE CONSUMER MARKET AND TO FAIR PRICES

Not the least among the rights and freedoms of the new economic system is the right of the consumer to have choices. The domestic consumer market today is almost totally destroyed, and, accordingly, our consumers — all of us — have no rights. Citizens of a great power have become hostages of empty shops and enslaved by production and distribution monopolies.

Among the many causes that have brought about this state of things, one of the most important is inflated money, which can't be spent as there are no goods to buy. The bulk of this money has been distributed to the population over the past several years. Recurrent talk about how this extra money is overhanging the economy, and somehow should be confiscated from the population, is immoral. Is it really possible to call these savings "extra" when they are not much more than a thousand and a half per capita? If we take into consideration the mostly scanty personal belongings of people, we realize that most people who have this extra money are not very far from the poverty threshold. Even the total sum of money the consumer is ready to pay now is extremely small. But even this weak monetary opposition is deadly for our consumer market.

We must normalize the consumer market through liberalizing pricing policy. During the transition period we will create commodities reserves, including import supplies, to encourage the coming gradual transition to free prices for many commodities. The exchange market will operate with a freely fluctuating rate of exchange. A number of major banks will get the right to sell foreign currency at market prices and Soviet citizens will be given the right to keep foreign currency freely in banks.

Some argue that a transition to a market economy is impossible without administrative price hikes. Our program, however, allows this transition without any centralized increase in prices. The market regulates price fluctuations. In the administrative system in the last few years prices have only risen. Our still nonmarket economy shows how life is rapidly becoming more and more expensive, and this is occurring more rapidly than the official statistics recognize.

Why should people trust Goskomtsen to come up with fair prices if it has never done so in the past? Certainly, there can be no guarantee that free market prices will immediately become fair, but with the market it will happen sooner or later. It never happens with the administrative system. Administrative control and centralized management of prices can never set adequate prices. Even when the government through administrative measures manages to keep prices low for this or that commodity (especially if the commodity is in shortage), the consumer's only consolation, as a rule, is the knowledge that these low prices exist somewhere. These commodities are not available in stores or they go to privileged strata of the population. Most consumers buy them at the market or on the black market at much higher than official prices.

Transition to free prices will be gradual and will start with goods which are not prime necessities and which mostly high-income people buy. Thus rising prices will mostly affect this upper strata of the population.

In accordance with this program, foodstuffs should be differentiated by their quality. Broad differentiation of prices for goods according to quality will go together with low prices for prime necessities. The share of free prices will gradually grow, as fast as the stabilization of the monetary system will allow. A special tax can be imposed on sales of high-quality foodstuffs to keep prices for necessities low. In no way can we begin the reform with the abolition of state subsidies for meat and dairy products. These subsidies should be preserved, but local soviets should be given the right to manage the most fair distribution of this assistance.

THE RIGHT OF CITIZENS TO GROWING INCOMES AND SOCIAL GUARANTEES

One of the most serious drawbacks of the existing system of state regulation of incomes and the living standard of the population is its rigidity. Minimum salaries, for example, have remained unchanged for decades. Over the too-long periods between revisions they lose their primary purpose. Moreover, the low incomes of the majority of the population set the primitive poverty-inspired policies. There were inadequate attempts to cover up negative processes in this sphere by uncoordinated measures, which were basically aimed at glossing over existing contradictions. Such an inability to respond quickly to changes in life is a typical feature of the existing system.

The market, a very mobile and flexible system, besides liberalizing economic processes, creates mechanisms to regulate changes in living standards. These changes include indexation of incomes and regular revisions of income levels in coordination with a system of social assistance to people who find themselves below the poverty level.

If we choose the market system, we are not necessarily in for a direct freeze on incomes, as both supporters and opponents of the market economy often predict. The program envisages a revival of the real dependance of earnings on the results of one's own effort with an obligatory, although not immediate, growth of the supply of goods. Only on this road can we achieve higher entrepreneurship and labor productivity, which, in its turn, will provide more possibilities for higher incomes.

Income on property is expected to increase. There will be higher interest rates for savings in banks, for state securities. There will also be income from shares.

There can be no social reorientation of the economy without a large-scale structural rearrangement. But no centralized administrative-and-command economic system can make it; nor can such a system satisfy all the needs of society. The structural rearrangement will require much effort and some sacrifices will be inevitable. But it is not the fault of the market, but rather is due to its absence. Without a structural rearrangement it will be impossible to bring about any considerable rise in living standards. Certainly, the closing down and restructuring of many industries will require temporary unemployment and the retraining of many people. In this way, however, a new and more effective structure of employment will form and hard and hazardous manual labor will decline. More skilled workers will earn more in new, effective jobs. The program envisages reorganization of the job placement service and the introduction of unemployment allowances. While between jobs, people can take part in public works like road and housing construction. Above all, they can participate in building their own homes. People can also get a plot of land and cultivate it.

There will be retraining programs and a system of voluntary public works will be organized. The acuteness of the unemployment problem is expected to ease as new jobs appear in new industries, in the trade and services sphere, and also in the newly developing private sector. The regulation of employment does not seek to guarantee a fixed job for every employee, but it seeks to ensure conditions for a constant perfection of skills and professionalism. It is the development and constant perfection of such a mechanism that will be the core of the state policy of employment.

THE RIGHT OF ENTERPRISES TO FREE ECONOMIC ACTIVITY

Economic freedom of enterprises means granting them the possibility to act in the interests of their employees, shareholders, and the state, and, according to the state of the market, to independently define the size and structure of production and sales and to set prices for their product as well as choose partners.

From the start, enterprises will be allowed to change ownership either by privatization (mostly small- and medium-sized firms) or transformation into stock companies (medium-sized and large). This means that work collectives, immediately after the program is announced, can start preparation and deal with this process in the least painful way, which will be fundamentally different from our usual practice of taking everybody unawares with such decisions. Enterprises will have a chance to choose top managers for themselves and hire them on a contract basis. To keep up economic stability the present economic ties will be, in all probability, frozen until July 1991. But immediately thereafter enterprises will attain the right to determine independently the volume and type of production, to choose their consumers and suppliers and to organize free distribution of their product across the country.

Enterprises will leave the system of branch monopolies and make contacts with their partners along a horizontal axis. They will also be able to purchase at the wholesale market material resources, including unfinished construction sites, and so on, freely sell extra equipment, raw materials, and other property, and borrow money. Enterprises will also be granted the right to participate directly in foreign economic activity and will be able to buy and sell currency on the domestic market.

While getting new rights and expanding their economic freedom, enterprises must be aware that the program envisages strict limitations for them: higher rates for credit, reduction of budget subsidies to zero, dramatic reduction of state capital investment, reduction of state purchases, and foreign competition. Enterprises must be aware of these realities in order to make better use of their new freedom.

THE RIGHTS OF THE REPUBLICS TO ECONOMIC SOVEREIGNTY

These rights are provided in accordance with the program on the basis of the Agreement on Economic Union of sovereign states and a number of other agreements, which supplement it. Some other agreements are expected, such as an agreement on interrepublic supplies, supplies for Union needs, and also on mechanisms to keep up economic relations during the transition period.

The basic idea in the relations between republics and the center is that nobody will guide, direct, and order anybody. The program is based on respect for the declarations of sovereignty adopted by the republics. Economic reform cannot be carried out through directions from the center, no matter how right they might be. People will no longer tolerate the most vital questions of their life being decided in the center without their participation. The program takes into account the skyrocketing of nationalist sentiment and gives the main role in the reform to republican governments and local authorities.

Realizing their rights to economic sovereignty, the people themselves will get a chance to deal with their national riches, prevent unreasonable squandering of resources and preserve nature for the coming generations.

Republic governments from now on will be responsible for the development of their territories and, accordingly, will have most economic powers.

The republics will set the main taxes, the forms and methods of privatization, and will regulate prices for most products. Each republic will determine its own land and housing reforms. Their governments will develop their own systems of social security and will independently draw up their republican budgets. The Union will get money to finance only programs that the people are really interested in.

The republics must determine the extent of their independence in managing the economy and take upon themselves management of certain types of state property. The final aim of delegating powers of state property management is not only to give it over to the republics, but to denationalize and privatize it in the long run. Many types of property are supposed to stay in the Union upon agreement among the republics.

Economic integration is necessary, and it must build upon voluntariness, mutual benefit, and equal partnership, but in no way on unitarism and dictatorship by the center. Entering the Economic Union, the sovereign states agree upon joint principles of economic policy, upon the development of a common market and reform coordination. The administration of the Union must have equal representation of all the republics. The powers, which will be delegated to the Union administration, are to be approved by all the republics and fixed in the Agreement on the Economic Union.

Participation in the Economic Union should be advantageous for the sovereign republics, thus the program must envisage the voluntary basis of their entering the Union and the right to freely leave the Union. But members of the Union must also take certain commitments upon themselves that are agreed upon by all the participants. In case a republic refuses to take on these commitments, but is willing to participate in some social and economic programs of the Union, the republic gets the status of associated participant (observer), which limits its rights in the Union.

THE ECONOMIC RIGHTS OF THE CENTER

Economic rights of the center are the rights delegated by the sovereign republics. Within the framework of these rights the center realizes its powers of managing All-Union property and funds, All-Union economic programs, and it also provides maximum possible coordination in the realization of the reform.

THE RIGHT OF SOCIETY

Our society has an indisputable right to live better right now, not in the far-off future, and the suggested program of transition to a market-oriented economy is aimed at the fullest possible realization of this right.

The task force is fully aware of the inadequacies of the suggested program, but we believe that events will result in its completion. We could not have done better, having limited information and only a month to work. We are grateful to the hundreds of experts, workers, scholars, and entire research institutes who supported this effort.

S. Shatalin, N. Petrakov, G. Yavlinsky, S. Aleksashenko, A. Vavilov, L. Grigoriev, M. Zadornov, V. Martynov, V. Machits, A. Mikhailov, B. Fedorov, T. Yarygina, E. Yasin.

August 1990
Moscow, Arkhangelskoe

PART I

THE CONCEPT OF THE PROGRAM FOR TRANSITION TO A MARKET ECONOMY AS THE FOUNDATION FOR AN ECONOMIC UNION OF SOVEREIGN REPUBLICS

1

The Socioeconomic Situation

CRISIS OF THE SYSTEM

The period of economic and political instability which the country is now undergoing must not be regarded as an ordinary, if severe, crisis that can be overcome by expending the internal reserves of the system. On the contrary, we are facing a general crisis in the socioeconomic system — including the national governmental structure, the economy, and ideology — a crisis that has exposed the nonviability of the existing order.

Up to a certain moment, this nonviability was concealed through extensive use of human and natural resources, but even this type of economic development had already been exhausted by the sixties. During the last two decades the rate of economic growth has declined continuously. The country's economy has not participated in the contemporary world's scientific and technological revolution. It proved to be lacking internal mechanisms for structural change. The gap in the level of technology, quality of goods, and living standards (where the difference is three to five times) between us and those countries having a developed market economy has reached a critical size.

Since the middle of the seventies the national economy has relied mainly on revenues from raw materials and energy export, on limitations on personal consumption, and on isolation from the world market. An economic growth of practically zero, and an "eating up" of the national wealth was observed in the eighties. Equipment in many industries has not been renovated for 15 to 20 years, fertility of the soil in a number of regions has decreased by a factor of two or three, natural resources have been used rapaciously, and environmental conditions in a number of regions have become substandard. A wretched quality of life for tens of millions of people, a shortage of the

**GROWTH RATES FOR NATIONAL INCOME (1) AND
INDUSTRIAL PRODUCTION (2) IN THE USSR 1975-1990**
(AS A PERCENT OF PREVIOUS YEAR)

major necessities, and a lack of material incentives to work have induced physical and social degradation.

The potential of today's socioeconomic crisis has accumulated for decades and could not fail to appear in acute, destructive forms. The coincidence of negative tendencies in the economy undergoing profound political reforms was inevitable. Socioeconomic contradictions were revealed openly during the democratization of the political system.

ECONOMIC POLICY IN 1985-1990

The direction of economic transformation (decentralizing, intensifying the motivation for work) chosen in 1985 was correct; however, the absence of a program for radical reform, the halfway nature of solutions, and the incompetence of the leadership of the managing bodies of the economy has only aggravated the crisis.

The monetary and financial policies of the government have been particularly harmful. Escalation of government expenditures combined with the

THE INTERNAL STATE DEBT OF THE USSR
(billions of rubles)

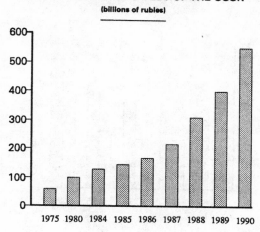

unchanged structure of production has led in actual fact to the liquidation of the consumer market. By 1985 a considerable potential for inflation had accumulated in the economy of the USSR, but due to the inflexible financial system it did not manifest itself. However, in the twelfth five-year plan period this potential sharply increased, and we can blame it on the incompetent and irresponsible administration of the financial institutions. While in 1981-1985 the reported internal state debt increased by 37.8 billion rubles, in the next five years it increased by more than 400 billion rubles. Taking into account that by the end of 1989 the net external debt of the USSR had more than doubled compared to the 1984 level, one can conclude that for the last ten years the country has been "living in debt" and is already on the brink of bankruptcy.

The policy of "acceleration," which envisaged the accelerated growth of plant and equipment within the framework of the old structure of priorities, has worsened the macroeconomic imbalance. Additional financial resources, received by increasing the monetary supply, were pumped into investments which were already hypertrophied. An overwhelming part of the additional capital investment became immobilized in unfinished construction and in ineffective production, arousing a mighty wave of inflation. Beginning with 1988 the situation in nonresidential construction can be characterized as an investment crisis, and additional subsidies cannot help to overcome it. Most significant is the decrease in the actual commissioning of construction

THE EXTERNAL HARD CURRENCY DEBT OF THE USSR

(billions of rubles)

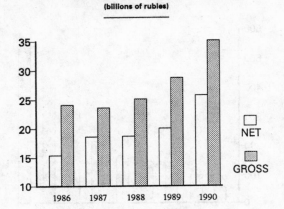

projects in the sociocultural sphere; plans for residential construction are also not being fulfilled.

Although centralized expenditures were sharply increased in the sociocultural sphere in order to raise the standard of living of the population, this, in fact, had the opposite effect because they were financed completely by increasing the money supply. Under these circumstances the nominal growth of personal incomes was immediately "eaten up" by inflation, and the shortage of consumer goods was simultaneously intensified (see Supplement).

The state budget suffered big losses as a result of the antialcoholic campaign and changes in world oil prices. Huge expenditures were required for the cleanup of technological catastrophes (Chernobyl) and natural calamities. An equally serious factor in destabilizing the financial system was the uncontrollable growth in the monetary funds for economic stimulation of enterprises, dating from the planned budget for 1986.

The funds for the development of production (FDP) increased at an extreme rate (almost ten times) during this period. The outstanding funds for material incentive (FMI) and for social development and residential construction (FSDRC) tripled. All markets experienced the pressure from these increases, especially the means of production. The main reason for this situation lies in the continuance of "weak market" budget constraints along with the government's refusal to draw down the uncommitted portion of enterprise profits.

GROWTH OF CAPITAL INVESTMENT

In ratio to growth of industrial production (1) and growth of commissioned fixed assets in ratio
to growth of capital investment (2) in the USSR.

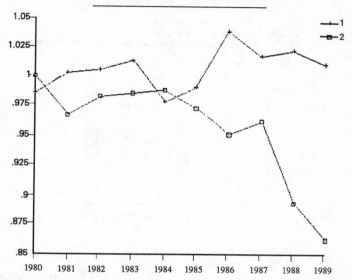

The inflationary financing of additional government expenditures coupled with the absence of objective statistical information made it possible to
support the illusion of favorable changes for some time. But this has made
social discontent even stronger now, in the period of the cruelest financial
crisis. In the present situation it is impossible to control the growth of the
money supply without extraordinary measures.

These errors in economic policy were made against a background of
inconsistent, halfway measures which changed isolated elements of the
existing economic system in ways that often merely touched the surface layer
of problems.

During a period of six months, the government proposed two totally
different programs of reform, neither of which commanded confidence, and
both turned out to be unsuitable for practical realization.

As paradoxical as it might seem, the period of 1985-1990 was objectively
necessary for society to become aware of the hopelessness of the existing
socioeconomic system and to elaborate a program of transition to a different
development model. Serious inertia in social development makes a period

ENTERPRISES FUNDS FOR ECONOMIC STIMULATION (FES)
(as of   January 1st) (Billions of rubles)

FDP ☐   (Fund for Development of Production)
FMI ▨   (Fund for Material Incentive)
FSDRC ▨ (Fund for Social Development and Residential Construction)

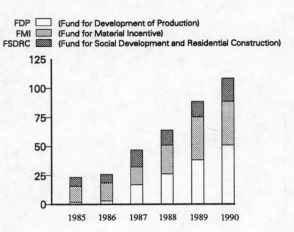

of "revision of old values" inevitable, but the ideas and knowledge accumulated during this period are essential for further reform.

The necessity to immediately determine the guidelines of economic reform and adopt a program of action and to begin implementing it is imposed by the following:

Since the end of 1988 the decrease in the growth rate of industrial production translates into an economic recession which is becoming worse with every month;

The financial situation is no longer under control; the budget deficit, the internal state debt, and the money supply are all accelerating;

The country's position in the world economy continues to worsen, the state remains solvent only by drawing down on its reserves which are steadily diminishing;

The consumer market has been almost entirely replaced by the black market and rationing, and social tension has reached the limit;

In the absence of a program of economic reform, government bodies of the republics, regions, districts, and enterprises are forced to search separately for ways out of this situation; as a result centrifugal tendencies arise and the crisis deepens.

GROWTH OF GNP AND MONEY SUPPLY (M₃)[1]

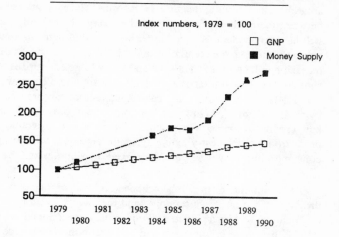

Index numbers, 1979 = 100

□ GNP
■ Money Supply

THE ALTERNATIVES

The acuteness of the economic and political crisis and of the national and ideological contradictions deprives the leadership of the country of the possibility of maneuvering and narrows the scope of any possible alternatives for further development. Today, for the political and economic center, there are only three alternatives from which to choose:

Follow the course of events, fighting negative processes after they have already gained strength. This is a policy of half-measures and gradual economic reform.

Accept the "reactionary" alternative, which calls for the restoration of the systems of centralized management of the economy (industry planning by directive, centralized allocation of material resources, strict income control, liquidation of all new forms of economic activity).

Accelerate the preparation and the implementation of radical economic reform, aiming within one and a half to two years to create the foundations for a market economy which is able to develop on its own and which is oriented to satisfy the needs of the people.

Let us examine the consequences of each scenario.

1. Gradual transformation. The possibility for this scenario is nearly exhausted because it leads to a continuation of the process of disin-

tegration of the economic system and the appearance of dozens of autarchies in regions and national territories. The exchange of goods between them will take the form of bartering. As a result, a choice will have to be made between hyperinflation and outright monetary confiscation from the population and the enterprises. The production recession will continue to deepen and many large enterprises will be shut down due to shortages in replenishing supplies. There will be a sharp deficit in consumer and capital goods that can only be offset by means of imports. However, the country will probably be denied new credits. A slump will begin in big cities and a decline in the productivity of the best-yielding agricultural regions will occur. The consumer market will be ousted by fixed distribution and the black market.

The economic crash will be deepened by the absence of a unified program of action. Each republic, and then every territory (up to a city district) will be trying to pull out of the crisis on its own, which will be disastrous in this integrated and overmonopolized economic system.

The political consequences of choosing this scenario will include the final collapse of the Union and the clashing of nationalities in the ethnically heterogeneous regions. Defiance of the law will embrace all spheres of life in society.

2. The scenario of a return to the economic system of a "1984 model" should be regarded as a realistic one, taking into account that it has many supporters both in the power structure and in certain groups of the population that have grown tired of unstable conditions of life. Many people are still unaware of the suicidal character of the old economic and political system that has pushed the country to the gutter of world progress. In the seventies to early eighties the crisis of a centrally planned economy continued to intensify, so a return would have to be made back to the economic system of the 1930's to the 1950's. Apparently, this will be impossible to achieve without large-scale political repressions, since the noneffectiveness of an overcentralized economy has been proven by the history of mankind.

3. Radical economic reform. The necessity to transfer to another type of social structure is dictated by the universal nature of the laws of economic and social development. Attempts to impose a different scenario, a unique path for one country, run counter to the logic of history and have been doomed from the start.

Meanwhile, today we have conditions favorable to radical transformations:

- the appreciation by a wide social strata of the essence of social processes, including economic ones, which have reached a level allowing for the elaboration and realization of a complex of reforms (political, economic, national-state structure);
- the enormous preparatory work for the last two to three years allows the elaboration, in a short period of time, of a detailed program of economic reforms, as well as the legislative acts, the practical and theoretical documents needed for its implementation;
- military confrontation has been eased, rational reordering of foreign economic relations and direct assistance to foreign countries permits formation of the reserves needed for a successful course of transformation.

However, the political will of the country's leadership is not sufficient for the success of any reform. The consent of the republics, the coordination of their actions, as well as the trust of the people, are essential.

2

The Goals of Reform and the Principles of the New Economic System

The principal aim of reform is to achieve economic freedom for the people and build an efficient business system on this base, which is capable of providing for the dynamic progress of the national economy, and the sufficient welfare of the citizenry, overcoming the lagging position with respect to other countries.

Mankind has not managed to create any system more efficient than a market economy. It gives strong incentives to materialize man's abilities, to activate labor and business, and to expedite greatly the progress of science and technology. Its own self-adjustment and self-regulation mechanism takes care of the best possible coordination of activities of all economic subjects, rationalizes the use of labor, material and financial resources, and balances the national economy. Obviously, transition to an economic system based on market relations is the only way to solve the country's most acute problems, to develop natural links between our economy and that of the world, to ensure the growth of production according to people's needs and thus the economy's social orientation, to eliminate shortages, and to make the achievements of world civilization accessible to our people.

A difficult, but necessary, turning point, essential to the country's future, would be reached with the replacement of state surveillance, parasitic smugness, wage leveling, apathy, and mismanagement — which were born of the command and administrative system — by free economic enterprise, each person's taking responsibility for his/her own welfare, intensive and well-arranged work, and remuneration according to the results.

The market is the only mechanism able to link different states and their economic systems. Therefore only market tools will enable the building of a voluntary union of sovereign republics within the framework of a renovated Union.

Certain conditions are prerequisite to a healthy market economy. These conditions should be developed in an interim period. They shall form the framework and principles of a new economic system.

1) Maximum **freedom for economic subjects** (an enterprise or an entrepreneur). This means a recognition of the important social role of the most active, qualified, and talented people — workers, farmers, owners or managers of production, and all kinds of incentives to entrepreneurship.

2) **Full responsibility of an economic subject** for the results of its business, based on legal recognition of all kinds of property, including private property. The notion of property actually implies the determination of full liability of the owner. In the course of further progress each type of ownership shall find its own most efficient place in the system, and the state should be relieved of functions that are not inalienable to it.

   It is only on the basis of new property relations that solutions can be found to problems of long-term interest to enterprises and individuals in finding the optimum proportions between consumption and accumulation, renewal and buildup of production potential, and improvement of efficiency of capital investments. Profit resulting from property rights is to be recognized as a legal source of income.

3) **Competition** of producers as a major source of incentive to business activities, improvement in the variety and quality of goods to meet market requirements, cost reduction and price stabilization. Promotion of healthy competition implies demonopolization of the economy, formation of an appropriate production structure that will provide for a sufficient number of suppliers of each and every commodity on the market, free operation of any economic individual on the market, state support of competition, and prevention of monopolistic practices.

4) **Market prices.** Market operations are possible only if the prevailing mass of prices emerge as a result of fluctuation, balancing supply and demand. State control of prices is only admissible in a limited sphere, without any violation of market pricing (which would lead to deficit).

5) **Market relations should be extended to all spheres** that are more efficient than state or other forms of regulations. Hence, the need to replenish the consumer goods market with labor and financial mar-

kets, which attribute higher flexibility and mobility to public resources and provide incentives to accumulation and progress of
science and technology.

Nevertheless, the economy shall retain a considerable nonmarket
sector comprising the activities that cannot be subject exclusively to
commercial criteria, such as defense, certain subsystems of health
care, education, science, and culture, et cetera.

6) **The economy of the USSR should be open** and consistently integrated into the world economic system. Every economic individual
should be granted the right to conduct external economic operations.
Foreign legal entities or physical persons may, on par with all and
any producers, operate on the domestic market according to existing
legislation and recognized international laws.

7) A major responsibility of state authorities at all levels, primarily at
republican and local ones, is to **provide a high standard of social
security** for the people. This is to be understood, on the one hand, as
a guarantee of equal opportunities for all people to earn their own
living, and on the other hand, as state support for disabled or socially
vulnerable people.

8) All **government bodies relinquish their direct engagement in
business** (with the exception of some special fields). While providing
for high economic efficiency of production, the market, however,
needs to be controlled by the state and public, in the sense that
negative uncontrolled consequences should be prevented. The latter
include unstable production, excessive differentiation in property or
social welfare, and uneven development of different regions. The
state should pursue a macroeconomic policy and assist in creating an
environment encouraging entrepreneurship, primarily in areas of
public interest.

A characteristic feature of the USSR, ensuing from its political structure
as a union of sovereign states, is that the main state responsibility for
economic regulation rests with the Union republics. All-Union and interrepublican bodies act on the authority delegated to them by the republics
under the terms of a new Union treaty; and the authority of local management
and management bodies is to be delegated to them by the republics in
accordance with their constitutions.

In pursuing its economic policy, the State shall use:

- legislative regulation of economic activities, including prevention of monopolistic policies, thereby encouraging healthy competition and protecting consumers and the environment;
- universal monetary and banking systems and regulation of the money supply;
- a system of taxes, incentives, and financial penalties;
- price control;
- budget allocation and operations with state-owned assets;
- goal-oriented social, economic, scientific, technological, and investment programs.
- Government control over economic activities shall be exercised within strict guidelines for legislative, executive, and judicial powers.

3

The Economic Union of Sovereign Republics[2]

The people's urge for economic and political sovereignty was expressed in the adopted Declaration on State Sovereignty (Independence) of the republics and in the legislative acts legalizing their economic independence.

Attempts to reverse the course of events have no future; sovereign republics hold it to be their common aim to radically change the unitary political, social, and economic structures.

At the same time, transformations in the national state structure of the USSR, although positive, are accompanied by acute conflicts and considerable economic losses. In a situation where neither All-Union authorities nor republican governments have the full power essential to pursue an economic policy, there is a great danger for an economy that functions as a centralized system.

Realizing the similarity of major problems of social and economic developments and taking into account the existing ties and relations in the field of production, financing, credit, trade, etc., as well as the need for coordinated efforts in the implementation of economic reforms, the sovereign states agree to establish a new Economic Union. This will enable them to put a stop to the disintegration of interrepublican economic links and to create new incentives for economic integration, based on the free will of all republics and with due regard for their interests.

The aims of the Economic Union are to provide for the welfare of all peoples, to promote and enrich the national cultures, and to implement the principles of human values by means of an efficient market economy and economic integration of the Republics, based exclusively on mutual interest and equal partnership.

The fundamentals of the Economic Union are as follows:

1. The Economic Union is based on equality of its members, which are sovereign states united voluntarily.

2. Entrepreneurs (owners, businessmen) and their enterprises are at the core of the economic system. Increasing their property increases the national wealth. The main role of the state in economic regulation is to pursue a macroeconomic policy, build the market infrastructure, and provide for the social security of the people.

3. The sovereign states, the members of the Economic Union, form a single, common, and universal economic environment and conduct a joint policy to shape the conditions for the free market activities of any business (enterprises, commercial organizations, or private persons) and for protection of the market.[3]

4. A Republic shall be admitted to membership in the Union provided it has accepted in full the obligations ensuing from the Treaty of Economic Union. A state which does not accept the obligations in full may be granted the status of an associated member, or of an observer, subject to the approval of all members of the Union. Members of the Union are free to quit. Member states violating the provisions of the treaty may be expelled from the Union.

THE ECONOMIC SOVEREIGNTY OF MEMBER-STATES OF THE UNION

Government regulation of economics shall be conducted by the Union republics, and the Union if authorized by the republics. Management bodies of the Economic Union shall act in accordance with the authority delegated to them by the republics.

The sovereign republics shall have exclusive right to legislative regulation of ownership, use and disposal of all national wealth on their territories. The earth and its minerals, inland and territorial waters, continental shelf, air space, and other natural resources, as well as the economic, scientific, and technological potential, are the property of the population of the republics and constitute the base of the republics' sovereignty. The sovereign republics are entitled to their share in the All-Union national wealth as of the date of signing of the treaty (including the diamond, currency and gold reserves of the Union).[4]

THE FUNCTIONS AND AUTHORITY OF THE
UNION MEMBERS

All functions and authority of Union members shall be based on the fundamental principle of the legislative supremacy of the sovereign republics and the effective distinction between functions of the republican and the All-Union administration. The sovereign states shall accordingly bear the main burden of responsibilities for the economic development of their territories, implement economic policies based on the separation of authority of the republics and of the Union, and shall independently build their own management structure for the economy of the nation.

The member-states of the Economic Union shall work out the fundamentals of a common economic policy and jointly define the legislation to govern the system of interrepublican relations, the procedures for dispute settlement, and conduct common pension and employment policies, and coordinate their social policies. Administrative bodies of the Union shall be set up for joint management and control of those spheres where a common economic policy is essential.

The republics shall, in the common interests of social and economic progress, delegate to the Union administrative bodies the authority to:

1. Provide the economic conditions required to support the defense of the Union, to ensure the security of the state, and to combat organized crime.

2. Elaborate long-term forecasts of the country's economic and social development and devise and implement large-scale programs for national economic development.

3. Implement common credit, financial, and monetary policies to consolidate the ruble's purchasing power. There shall be no restrictions on money flow within the Union.

4. Elaborate and adopt common customs regulations to protect the All-Union market. No quotas, restrictions, or customs barriers shall be allowed within the Union for goods defined by interrepublican agreement.

5. Control and regulate prices for certain raw materials, products, goods, and services itemized in an agreement signed by all members of the Economic Union.

6. Adopt a common foreign trade strategy to establish and use the All-Union Currency Fund to meet the obligations of the USSR to the international community.

7. Elaborate and conduct All-Union ecological programs.

**SHARE OF REPUBLIC PRODUCT CONSUMED
OUTSIDE THE REPUBLIC**

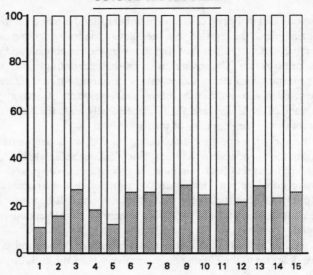

REPUBLICS:

1. Russia	9. Moldavia
2. Ukraine	10. Latvia
3. Byelorussia	11. Kirgizia
4. Uzbekistan	12. Tajikistan
5. Kazakhstan	13. Armenia
6. Georgia	14. Turkmenistan
7. Azerbaijan	15. Estonia
8. Lithuania	

8. Elaborate and conduct All-Union programs in social security and welfare.

9. Arrange common patents and licenses, meteorology, weights and measures services; introduce All-Union and international standards; arrange All-Union statistics and a common accounting system.

10. Manage activities that require unified management on the national level, namely:

   - fundamental research;
   - the defense programs;
   - the common power supply system;

SHARE OF CONSUMER PRODUCTS PRODUCED OUTSIDE THE REPUBLIC

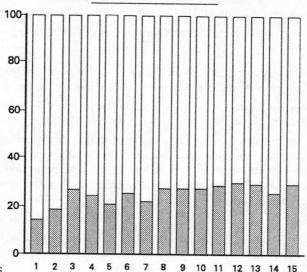

REPUBLICS: 1 2 3 4 5 6 7 8 9 10 11 12 13 14 15

1. Russia
2. Ukraine
3. Byelorussia
4. Uzbekistan
5. Kazakhstan
6. Georgia
7. Azerbaijan
8. Lithuania
9. Moldavia
10. Latvia
11. Kirgizia
12. Tajikistan
13. Armenia
14. Turkmenistan
15. Estonia

- the main-line railways and pipelines;
- the nuclear power industry;
- the space systems and space research;
- the All-Union systems of communication, information, and computer technology;
- the All-Union system of dealing with emergency situations.

State bodies managing maritime transport, the (deep-sea) fishing fleet, and air transport shall surrender their authority to new transrepublican joint-stock companies. Similar companies may be set up in other spheres upon agreement of the republics.

Pursuing common objectives, the sovereign republics together shall form joint property (All-Union property). Special agreement shall define the scope and management rules of All-Union property.

Union and republican authorities should observe the following rules:

1. Authority delegated to the Union administrative bodies may not be changed without the agreement of all members of the treaty.

2. Members of the treaty shall bear economic responsibilities for breach of their obligations.

3. Authority delegated to Union bodies shall provide for uniform regulation of the economic regime on the basis of antitrust legislation, common measures against unfair competition, protection of consumer interests, regulation, and leveling of starting conditions of the republics in their market transition.

This treaty and the legislative acts and rules thereunder shall be the legal ground for new economic relations among the sovereign republics.

THE UNION ADMINISTRATIVE BODIES

The structure of the Union bodies may follow the principle of equal representation for all republics, or the principle of a federation, subject to their nature.

MEMBERSHIP IN THE ECONOMIC UNION

Membership in the Economic Union is open to any republic that recognizes the founding principles and respective obligations.

If a sovereign state does not accept certain obligations agreed upon by all Union members, it shall have the status of an associated member (observer) of the Economic Union and shall be entitled to participation in specific All-Union programs, if it has contributed its share to the financing of these programs.

If a republic declares its wish to secede from the Economic Union, its government shall give advance notice to all members of the Union. The seceding republic shall in this case guarantee the compensation of its debts and fulfillment of its former obligations.

THE UNION BUDGET

The procedure to form and use the budget of a sovereign republic shall be defined by the legislation of that republic. It is free to work out independently and employ its own system of taxation, dues, and compulsory payments. All business and legal or physical persons in the territory of a republic shall make their payments (deductions, deposits, etc.) to the republican and local budgets only.

The Union budget shall be based on the contributions of the Union republics, enabling the Union to exercise its delegated authority. The amount to be contributed shall be defined on the basis of the GNP of the respective republic or on a GNP per capita basis. Coordination of the amount of a republic's contribution to the Union budget and of the GNP per capita is aimed at leveling the starting conditions for the transition to market relations for all members of the Economic Union. Upon agreement of the republics, the contribution may be collected in the form of federal taxes.

The Union budget shall stipulate the following expenditures (itemized in arbitrary order):

- defense;
- state security;
- combating organized crime;
- large-scale actions for environmental protection;
- social and other special programs on the All-Union scale;
- funding for regional development (and state subventions);
- a fund for emergencies, etc., and elimination of the damage done by calamities and natural disasters;
- repayment of the USSR domestic and external state debts and interest on it;
- the Union's external economic activities;
- maintenance and upkeep of the Union's administrative bodies;
- financing fundamental scientific research;
- a reserve fund.

The republics which are members of the Economic Union, as per mutual agreement, may finance the budget fulfillment as well as other economic, scientific and technical, social and ecological programs on the basis of the bilateral or multilateral principles.

THE HARD-CURRENCY FUND OF THE UNION

The Currency Fund will be created by the republics to finance the foreign economic activity of the Union subject to its responsibility and will be formed on the basis of financial contributions of the republics, the amount of which will be specified on the basis of shares of the republic in the above fund. The amount of the fund will be specified out of the necessity to cover the following expenses in hard currency:

1. Settling the state external debt of the USSR. For this purpose, the amount of such debt, as well as the approved and agreed-upon share of it, for each republic will be fixed on a date to be specified in the agreement. (The settling of the state external debt of the USSR will be effected by all the republics in the agreed order. The total amount will be fixed by the state on a date to be specified in the agreement. The share of the associated members of the Union and the order of settling the debt will be specified).

2. All new debts will be handled either jointly or separately. In the first case the debt will involve expenses connected with settling the external debt of the Union. In the second case, the debt will be considered as the state external debt of the corresponding republic and the expenses connected with its reimbursement will be the responsibility of the republic.

3. Granting of loans and rendering other economic aid to foreign states, as well as the conclusion of the agreements for receiving such aid from foreign sources on behalf of the Union, may be done on the basis of agreement of all the republics.

4. The fulfillment of external economic obligations and the obligations connected with installments for international organizations, banks, and funds will be effected in the order specified in paragraphs 1 and 2.

5. Imports required for achieving general programs, keeping institutions abroad, and certain other expenses, will be effected according to the requirements of the above expenses and should be paid by the republics in equal shares.

The All-Union currency reserves will be held on a level required for settling the existing external debt of the USSR and new All-Union programs.

THE ECONOMIC UNION AND THE REFORM

The independent member-states of the Union see no other way to overcome the crisis of the social and economic system but by introducing an economic reform to establish a market economy.

The members note that it is impossible to improve the current economic situation using the old system of administration of the economy of the USSR. The administrative bodies of the Union should correspond to the principles of the Economic Union.

Each sovereign republic will independently determine the set of measures for transition to the market on the basis of an agreed and approved conception. Taking into account specific conditions, the republics will define the most effective usage of economic potential, perform a structural reorganization, and create the basic market establishments. Nevertheless, the success of the economic reform will require coordination of the actions taken by individual republics.

The program of transition to a market economy should be considered as a basis for coordinated action of the member-states of the Economic Union. Standard drafts of the legislative and normative acts to be worked out under this program can be used as models for corresponding legislation of the republic. To accomplish the program, the Interrepublican Economic Committee will be established, subordinate to the President of the USSR.

SUPPLEMENTARY AGREEMENTS TO THE
AGREEMENT OF ECONOMIC UNION

Simultaneously with conclusion of the agreement for creation of an Economic Union, the members will sign a series of agreements on forms and methods of coordinating economic policy of the member-states of the Union. These agreements should cover:

1. Setting up the reserve system of the Union and establishing a common monetary policy.
2. The budget of the Union.
3. The fiscal system.
4. The customs policy of the Union.
5. The hard-currency fund of the Union, the foreign exchange policy.
6. The deliveries and the work to be done for the mutual needs of the Union.
7. Interrepublic commerce.
8. The pension fund of the Union.
9. The employment fund of the Union.

4

The Logic and Stages of the Transition to a Market Economy

THE GENERAL CONCEPT

The transition from a command economy to a market economy has its own internal logic, which must be respected for this process to be successful.

On the one hand this process involves radical institutional changes which will affect the entire system of social and economic relations and the production structure. On the other hand it requires stabilization primarily in the monetary and financial fields and in the sphere of price setting.

Reform efforts should be concentrated on the following tasks:

1) Denationalizing of the state economy, privatizing and the development of entrepreneurship. Denationalizing of the economy is understood as a process by which the state is removed from direct control over economic units, that corresponding rights and responsibilities be passed to the enterprise level, that horizontal links between individual enterprises be substituted for vertical ones. All this can be done without any change in ownership.

Privatizing the economy implies concession (transfer or sales under various conditions of state property to the economic agents, who shall have the authority to use it in their economic activity and bear full material responsibility for the results obtained). Denationalizing and privatizing assert commercial discipline on firms and their financial self-sufficiency and as such can be regarded as important cures for the ailing financial system. Furthermore, denationalizing and privatizing the economy shall guarantee the development of entrepreneurship and improve the economic position of the USSR by permitting our vast reserves to be put into the economic turnover. (An entrepreneur, who is one of the key figures in any market economy, misses no opportunity to identify idle resources and put them to work.)

2) Development of the market and market infrastructure, introduction of new mechanisms for establishing economic ties, and promotion of entrepreneurship. In the most important sectors of the economy, the system of state contracts and centralized allocation of limited amounts of goods produced under such contracts shall remain in force during all of the transition period, at least for basic economic products. Such contracts shall help to balance material flows of basic goods in the period of rapid economic change, but special measures should be taken to limit their scope so they do not hinder market development.

3) Demonopolizing the economy and abolishing the institutional framework that has been formed under the command system and today stands in the way of development of a market. The successful fulfillment of these tasks is the most important prerequisite for development of entrepreneurship, market competition, and transition to free prices.

4) The gradual removal of the state's control over prices and transition to free pricing based on the patterns of supply and demand, without which a market mechanism cannot function.

5) Conducting austere monetary and financial policies to limit the amount of money in circulation. The need for such policies is determined by the fact that inflation of the money supply and shortage of goods are inseparable attributes of the command system. Without austerity measures the removal of state control over prices will lead to extremely high rates of inflation.

6) The creation of a strong system of social support and social guarantees, which would help people to adapt to the conditions of the market economy and protect the socially vulnerable strata of the population from the stresses of the transition period.

7) Conducting an active investment policy. Investment policy should be based primarily on economic incentives and its principal aim should be to bring about the necessary structural shifts in the national economy, the accelerated growth of consumer goods and services, the reduction of losses, and increased production flexibility with sensitivity to demand and technology changes.

In the last analysis, structural reorganization is a prerequisite of market equilibrium and market efficiency.

The implementation of each of these tasks requires accelerating the creation of appropriate legal foundations, and will take a significant amount of effort at all levels of the state political administration structure.

Fulfilling these tasks will require much more than a team of experts who have a ready answer for every question, who patronize everyone and give orders. The essential thing about the market is that it is a self-evolving system that results from the activities of millions of individuals and requires no special planning. It is this last consideration that is the key to success of the program of transition to a market economy.

The aim of the program is simply to direct this activity and to minimize the economic and social losses that are inevitable in the period of transition. The practical steps to be taken should be selected and coordinated accordingly.

The proposed outlines of the reform and the sequence of steps to be taken reflect an understanding of the fact that the transition to a market economy, which starts with the launching of the program and continues until the market gains its full momentum, is a relatively long process involving radical structural reorganization of the national economy and dramatic changes in the attitudes and behavior of millions of people.

However, we realize that the time for gradual reforms has been missed, that partial reforms proved ineffective both in our country and in countries of Eastern Europe. The economic and national crisis, the discontent of people, and the loss of hope for change for the better require immediate, decisive, and comprehensive actions to bring the situation under control.

World experience shows that all successful stabilization policies are short-term and as a rule are triggered off by monetary and financial reforms.

Hence the first phase of the proposed reform scenario centers around the improvement of the monetary system while maintaining the existing economic ties and material flows within the economy. Without a stable ruble it would be impossible to stimulate production, to increase economic turnover, and to introduce market prices. A hard ruble will have the immediate effect of balancing the supply and demand for goods, of saturating the market, and will serve as a starting point for action along other lines.

The first emergency steps in this sphere should be followed by a complex of coordinated medium- and long-term measures. Hence the next step after achieving noticeable results in the financial and monetary sphere should be the liberalization of prices, taking care to do this while taking into account changing socioeconomic conditions.

Parallel to this, active measures should be taken to denationalize and demonopolize the economy, to promote entrepreneurship and market competition so as to create, in the shortest possible time, the prerequisites for market self-regulation. Only market regulation can ensure stabilization of prices, stimulate growth and diversification of production, improve quality and reduce losses.

Until market forces come into action the state should conduct an austere financial policy to prevent the risk of unmanageable inflation. Such a policy, however, may have a negative effect in curtailing business activity and hindering production.

Consequently structural reorganization of the economy should be narrowed down to a small list of only the most urgent steps.

This period of austere financial policy, price liberalization, denationalization and demonopolization of the economy will be the period of economic stabilization. It will continue until there are unequivocal signs of market competition and self-regulation.

Immediately after the implementation of the program will come a period of development of a full-fledged market, of an active investment policy, and a rise in production and an improvement in efficiency.

Unlike all previous reform models, the present program takes into account the emergence of an unprecedented political situation. With the declarations of the sovereignty of the republics, a common centralized program for all the republics would no longer work. Each republic is able to choose and conduct its own program of economic reform on the basis of an analysis of the socioeconomic, national, and cultural peculiarities of local conditions. In fact, the process of reform has already taken this course. Common goals and common problems facing the republics, and the technological and financial ties existing between them, dictate the necessity of coordinating individual republican reform programs with the general transition plan. The republican decision makers shall choose their policy independently, but on the basis of common principles. Coordination and synchronization in the implementation of republican programs in time will contribute to the success of the reform and reduce possible losses.

The suggested action plan was compiled so as to satisfy the economic interests of each republic and to carefully specify all instances of All-Union intervention. The action plan makes provision for the coordination on the scale, form, and pace of republican reforms and for laying the economic foundation for the future system of interrelationships that will exist between the republics.

Along most of the lines of economic reform, the republics shall act on their own on the basis of economic sovereignty and horizontal coordination. The list of the tasks which can be solved on the republican level is as follows:

- denationalization and privatization of the economy, promotion of entrepreneurship;
- demonopolization of the economy and reorganization of the existing institutional structures;
- investment policy oriented toward structural change;
- regulation of incomes and social support of the population.

However, there are tasks which would take a centrally coordinated effort to implement. Among them are:

- monetary, financial, and foreign exchange policies;
- extraordinary measures for limiting the money supply and overcoming the budget deficit;
- liquidation of state control over prices;
- reorganization of foreign trade.

The policy of structural change will also require a certain coordination of measures taken in structural policy and the promotion of state regulation of production through the system of state contracts.

There is no time to be lost. The suggested action plan, for which the government of the country can still receive a vote of confidence, will take only 500 days or so to implement, and during this time it must institute reforms that will clear the way for development of the market, radically improving in a visible manner the economic situation and living standards of the people.

THE FIRST 100 DAYS — A PROGRAM OF EXTRAORDINARY MEASURES
(OCTOBER 1, 1990 — BEGINNING OF 1991)

First day — the President of the USSR and the leaders of the republics declare the introduction of legislative acts laying down the foundations for the main principles of the economic reform:

- establishing equal rights of physical and legal subjects to engage in any kind of economic activity not prohibited by law;

- denationalizing the state economy, transferring dwellings and available lands from the state to the population (through concessions or sales), reorganizing large state enterprises into joint-stock companies; privatizing small shops, public catering and consumer services;
- establishing the guarantees of ownership rights for physical and legal subjects (both Soviet and foreign) with respect to all kinds of property, except in certain cases where the government shall have exclusive property rights;
- excluding articles that define penalties for entrepreneurial activity from the criminal and administrative codes and granting amnesty for those who have been sentenced under these articles. This action should be paralleled with the enforcement of laws against property violations and measures that ensure the maintenance of law and order;
- conferring on the President of the USSR and on the top administration of the national republics emergency powers to conduct reform in the monetary and financial spheres.

The program of transition to a market economy shall be implemented under the supervision of the Interrepublican Economic Committee to be created under the auspices of the President. The Committee shall be invested with full power to exercise efficient and flexible control over the reform process.

We recommend that the Supreme Soviet of the USSR and the Supreme Soviets of Union Republics put aside all other legislative drafts and adopt the set of acts pertaining to market transition before the end of 1990. If the said acts are not adopted in due time, they shall be put temporarily into action by the decrees of the President of the USSR.

The inventory of State property, financial assets, and reserves of all kinds shall be accompanied by the transfer of property rights from the state to the public. This transfer could take the following forms:

1. Sales of state-owned cars and trucks.
2. Auctions of uncompleted construction projects which were financed out of the state budget; auctions of uninstalled equipment and construction materials.
3. Sales of stocks of goods of general civil value.
4. Returning to the state the property of public organizations which was financed out of the state budget (through assertion of relevant claims).

This property shall then be sold to enterprises and individuals.

By the end of the current year 50 to 60 state enterprises shall be reorganized into joint stock companies. Certain categories of dwellings and lands shall be ceded to private owners either free of charge or against symbolic payment. Small shops and other small enterprises shall be leased or rented out. The State Property Committees shall start preparing the grounds for the privatization of large state enterprises.

The republics shall declare the fundamentals of land reform:

The workers of collective and state farms shall have the right to their individual shares of land within their borders; all lands shall be reregistered; the right to quit a collective farm with his share of land and other property shall be guarantied to all farmers. Lands inefficiently used by their present owners shall be expropriated and offered to private farmers.

An important step at this phase shall be the creation of a market infrastructure for purchases, storage, processing, and sale of agricultural products and the establishment of land banks.

Resolute measures shall be taken to restore normal functioning of the financial and monetary systems. Within the first hundred days it will be necessary to reduce the deficit of the state budget to 5 billion rubles (fourth quarter of 1990) and to achieve a zero growth rate for the total money supply. This will require revision and review of all articles on the expense side of the budget of the Soviet Union and the national republics, and the enactment of extraordinary measures to reduce budget expenditures. The financial austerity and discipline which will be adopted at the end of the current year should be reflected in the Union, republican, and local budgets for 1991.

All forms of external aid (except for humanitarian aid shall be reduced by at least 75 percent.

The budget of the Ministry of Defense and the KGB should be reduced by 10 to 20 percent. Such a reduction shall be achieved through the reduction of state purchases of arms and military construction while maintaining the present level of salaries and wages set in the production plans. This will also allow for savings of raw material which shall be sold in the market.

At least 30 percent of the gains achieved due to cutting expenses shall be used for financing the increased salaries of army officers and for residential construction for military personnel, including those who have been transferred back to the USSR and retired officers.

Production investments financed out of the state and republican budgets shall be reduced and uncompleted projects in the early phases of construction shall be suspended with the exception of those intended for consumer goods production, residential construction, and social development purposes. All uncompleted construction projects shall be officially registered.

No budget program exceeding 100 million rubles will be adopted for 1991 except those to alleviate the consequences of Chernobyl. All budgetary items exceeding the limit of 100-500 million rubles must be passed for approval by the Supreme Soviet of the USSR and the Supreme Soviets of the Union republics on a case-by-case basis.

All state subventions and subsidies to enterprises shall be canceled starting from January 1, 1991.

The state shall also make an attempt to sell part of the debts of other countries to the USSR on the world market.

All these and other measures are aimed at mobilizing the reserves of the state as a source of financing the transition to a market economy. Only when all the possibilities in this respect have been exhausted and the people acknowledge this fact will the government have the right to appeal to the people to show patience, confidence, and solidarity in getting the country out of crisis.

Not later than October 15 the State Bank of the USSR and all affiliates shall be transformed into the Reserve System of the Soviet Union, comprising the central banks of all Union republics.

The banks of the Reserve System shall be legally denied the right to finance budgetary expenses. The budget deficit shall be financed out of sales of state securities on reasonable terms.

In force-majeure circumstances the President of the USSR shall have the right to allow the Reserve System of the Union to grant the Ministry of Finance a short-term (12 months) credit not exceeding 5 billion rubles.

The state shall issue special reform bonds to be sold to the population and abroad. The bonds shall have a payment term of three years and their amount shall not exceed 10-15 billion rubles.

Within the first 100 days all specialized banks of the state shall be transformed into joint-stock commercial banks. It is possible, however, that one state bank will be preserved. Supported by the budget this bank could grant credits on favorable terms and stimulate business activity in the interests of the state.

Interest rates on loans and deposits will start rising. Eventually, money will get more "expensive", thus obtaining a necessary property for circulation within a market economy.

In November a stock exchange will be opened in Moscow.

Before December 1, 1990, the balance sheets of state banks shall be divided: all transactions shall be passed through correspondent accounts. The subdivision of bank balances will enable the transition to a normal mechanism of cash emission through the sale of bank notes against bank money.

This will enable the introduction of financial instruments for controlling the amount of credit granted.

From the beginning of 1991 money circulation shall be subject to regulation.

By that time many enterprises will already have encountered financial difficulties due to fixed wholesale prices and shortages with respect to the means of circulation. These difficulties would be especially grave for enterprises with extensive credit financing as compared to the self-financed enterprises. In order to facilitate the adjustment of enterprises to the new environment, to give them a chance to accumulate their own means of circulation and to improve their performance, the following steps shall be taken:

- privatization and transformation of low-performance enterprises into joint stock companies; large state enterprises shall be split into smaller firms;
- establishing stabilization funds;
- promoting commercial credit, which is seen as an element of the new wholesale market, and reducing the demand for bank credit;
- stimulating the issuing of bonds as a source for replenishing the means of circulation;
- closing down 100 to 200 money-losing enterprises.

The instability of market ties evolving in the early stages of reform and the risk of economic chaos shall dictate certain measures to stabilize material flows within the production sphere. These measures include the following:

1. The existing economic ties will be unconditionally maintained until July 1, 1991. All previous contracts between enterprises and agreements concluded at the interrepublican level shall remain in force, and strict sanctions shall be introduced for the violation of the said contracts and agreements. The representatives of many republics insisted on unconditional preservation of all economic ties until the end of 1991, but such a solution does not seem very realistic. State contracts shall indeed be maintained in many cases, but by preserving all the existing contractual ties we would run the risk of hindering market development and the free exchange of commodities between enterprises.

2. In 1990-1991 certain enterprises previously closed for polluting the environment shall be temporarily reopened, provided that their produce is necessary to maintain the production of socially important commodities.

   The allocation of material and technical goods covered by state contracts for the year 1991 shall be handled through the State contracting system — a new entity which shall replace the present Gossnab (State Committee for the Allocation of Resources), The Ministry of Trade and Agrosnab (State Committee for Allocating Resources to the Agricultural Sector). All other goods shall be marketed between enterprises either directly (direct contracts) or through intermediation (commercial wholesale trade).

3. In 1991 the wholesale and retail prices, along with the norms and coefficients, suggested by the State Committee on Prices of the USSR shall be considered null and void. The scope shall be widened for negotiating prices of state contracts and for free prices in the wholesale trade. Products manufactured by the monopolistic enterprises shall be liable to state control. The goods produced under state order shall be sold at prices that the state shall negotiate with manufacturers, major consumers, and the wholesale trade organizations. The prices for basic fuel and raw material resources shall be fixed by the state on the basis of multilateral negotiations among the republics and will be considered obligatory for all the manufacturers.

4. The state shall renounce the policy of raising retail prices administratively. In 1991 state control over retail prices shall be gradually removed; the prices of basic necessities shall, however, remain at their present level.

5. Special attention shall be devoted to the stable functioning of transportation. The railways shall come under special state-of-emergency regulation.

6. The rapid development of a market infrastructure shall be a task of top priority; in 1991 the market should become the principal instrument for regulating commodity streams.

7. A system of taxation for enterprises shall be introduced from January 1, 1991. In order to adopt timely budgets for 1991, the existing system of state taxes shall be used until the end of 1990 (with minor adjustments by the republics).

8. A coherent system of hard-currency retentions shall be introduced. The system of quotas and licensing of import-export operations and

external borrowing shall be revised and the republican share in foreign trade operations shall be considerably increased.

From November 1, a single rate of ruble exchange shall be used both for commercial and noncommercial operations. The system of differentiated hard currency coefficients shall be abolished.

The protection of the ruble as the only legal means of payment within USSR territory shall be ensured. All forms of trade in foreign currency will be prohibited. At the same time measures shall be taken to develop the hard currency market. Not less than five to ten large banks shall be granted the right to perform transactions in hard currency using hard currency market prices. Soviet citizens shall be granted the right to own Western currencies and foreigners shall be allowed to open ruble bank accounts.

9. The above measures shall create favorable conditions for increasing consumer-goods production and services. Additional sources of economic growth shall be provided by conversion of defense industries, leases and sales of small industrial, trade, and service enterprises to individuals and granting privileges and credits on favorable terms to the new owners.

10. Measures shall be taken to restrain the increase of personal incomes; the existing income tax regulations shall remain in force until the end of 1990.

Preparatory works shall be conducted to set up a social security system and employment offices and organize statistical control over the dynamics of prices.

The republics shall devise and put into action systems of indexing incomes (starting date: December 1, 1990).

11. To avoid the uncontrollable growth of demand and at the same time to curb the risk of inflation, which will run high with the liberation of prices, measures shall be taken to stabilize the consumer market.

These measures include the following:

1) The deposit rates of the savings bank shall be increased;
2) Some state property (cars, military materials with civilian use) shall be sold off;
3) Some construction facilities previously used in industrial construction shall be used in residential construction and financed out of revenues from sales of state-owned apartments. Construc-

tion materials withdrawn from industrial construction shall be redistributed;

4) Construction of garages for privately owned cars shall be increased;

5) Additional land for the construction of summer houses shall be allocated;

6) Insurance service shall be developed; new kinds of insurance services shall be offered to the public;

7) The structure of imports shall change; the share of consumer goods shall be increased. Nontraditional channels shall be used in order to minimize the risk of abuse in the distribution of imported goods.

It is necessary to accumulate the required reserves of commodities until the end of the period of extraordinary measures. The sources for accumulating said reserves shall be found in restricting the limited-access sales (i.e., sales organized exclusively for the workers in a given enterprise) and in foreign aid.

12. New customs tariffs shall be introduced to improve the terms of trade and restrict the volume of foreign trade operations based on quotas and licensing.

The measures to be taken during the first 100 days presuppose that the budget deficit shall be cut down to the planned level and that the measures directed to keeping the amount of money in circulation under control shall be successful. The success of the proposed reform plan will also depend on the coordinated actions of the Union republics and on the confidence of the population. If these conditions are satisfied, it would be possible with the help of relatively "soft" measures to shift the USSR economy to a different stage and to prepare for transition to a market economy within a short period. However, if the said conditions are not met, austere and painful measures shall be required.

THE 100TH TO 250TH DAYS: LIBERALIZATION
OF PRICES WITH AUSTERE FINANCIAL CONSTRAINTS

When the extraordinary measures of the first 100 days are realized, the national economy will change substantially. People, as well as enterprises and organizations in most spheres of the national economy, will find themselves existing under new conditions.

The principal task of the second stage is to maintain the achieved results, to facilitate the adaptation to new conditions, to systematically increase the positive potential of reform, to create favorable conditions for promoting a full-fledged market.

The main aim of this stage is to remove state control over prices of the majority of manufacturing and technical equipment, consumer goods and services, and to keep inflation under control using financial and credit policy. In the course of this stage, the budget deficit should be reduced to zero and the money supply should not be allowed to grow. Simultaneously, denationalization should be expanded, small enterprises should be privatized, and the market infrastructure should be intensively developed.

The first result of the extraordinary measures and liberalized prices should be a considerable improvement in the consumer market, and in particular with respect to goods available at prices determined by supply and demand. Prices will be higher than existing state ones, but much lower than the prices on the black market. The rise in prices will be smaller if the monetary and fiscal policies are rigidly adhered to and succeed in removing excess demand. Consumer goods will appear in the market and be freely available for purchase. This is the first positive result of the reform we can expect, and we should do our best to achieve it.

An important role will be played by the increase in the volume of distributed consumer goods purchased with reserves and with the help of foreign aid. Of considerable importance is the rational distribution of goods with respect to the timing of their appearance and the area of the country of their utilization. Special channels of delivery and storing of goods should be arranged.

At the end of the first half of 1991, indexation of income in accordance with the dynamics of retail prices will be implemented. If the price index is higher than a certain level, income indexation will be started at the end of the first quarter.

Due to the introduction of a new tax system, rising interest rates on loans, and monetary restrictions, manufacturers may experience a currency shortage and have difficulties in selling their products. This will make them pay more attention to their customers' demands, particularly in the field of nonmonopolized production, to keep existing links with permanent customers. When resources are purchased at market prices, bartering will end.

The possibility of a reduction in the volume of production in some branches should be taken into account.

During the first months of this stage, work will be completed on the distribution of state orders and the resultant products for the third to fourth quarters of 1991.

The removal of administrative control over prices of the next groups of goods should be done by taking into consideration the actual situation of the market and has to be accompanied by financial and credit regulations. Further measures directed toward reduction of the budget deficit will be undertaken. Transfer of a considerable amount of revenue from the budget of the Union to the republics and local budgets will oblige them to decide how to it should be utilized, either to continue the scale of subsidy payments or to reduce them, thus freeing prices, while compensating the population for the price rises through a system of indexation or by other methods.

The republics and the local authorities may use a temporary price freeze for consumer goods if they rise excessively, or even introduce a system of rationing of some goods. In this case the producers and the retail trade will be compensated from the government budget for the losses they suffer.

A policy to denationalize and demonopolize the economy and stimulate private business should be carried out energetically.

The republican committees and the Union fund of state property will speed up the process of denationalization. The number of joint-stock companies to be created from large state enterprises will number 1000 to 1500 at the end of this stage. The selling off of shares of converted enterprises will be speeded up, and will be used for paying off the state debt. Besides joint-stock companies, the spinoff of state property may take other forms. For example, one-time repurchase, sale with the payment in installments, lease with the option to buy, or foreign investment.

Decentralization and privatization should be concerned particularly with trade, public food supply, and services. In the above sectors, first of all, state monopolies should be liquidated and conditions for competition should be created. The possibility of abuses when distributing assets, including the creation of artificial deficits, should be anticipated by the creation of a system of harsh economic actions and legal responsibility, including criminal responsibility.

At the end of this stage the different forms of private enterprise cover up to 50 percent of small food shops, nonfood stores, and other kinds of shops and public eating establishments.

Simultaneously the process of abolishing the outmoded administrative structures should be speeded up, as well as the reorganization of monopolistic enterprises and associations created as horizontally integrated units whose technological interconnections are not constrictive.

By the spring of 1991 the first stage of agrarian reform should be completed.

One may presume that while employees will seek compensation for the rise in prices, the enterprises will strive to respond by increasing their income with no change in production. The risk of social conflict may force enterprises to agree to workers' demands. This will increase inflationary pressures.

In order to avoid such circumstances, a public agreement should be reached on wage control and on having a set package of measures to control monetary aggregates. Such measures can be instituted by the President of the USSR through his emergency powers.

THE 250TH TO 400TH DAYS: MARKET STABILIZATION

On the whole, the principal task of this stage is to reach market stabilization for consumer goods and the means of production. Likewise, we should widen market relations and arrange a new system of economic relations.

The intensive process of decentralization continues. Before the 400th day, up to 30 to 40 percent of industrial capital assets, up to 50 percent of construction and motor transport facilities, and not less than 60 percent of trade, public feeding, and services should be transformed into joint-stock companies, sold or leased. The former system of enterprise management will be transformed as the new property relationships emerge.

Antimonopoly activity will be strengthened. On the basis of the adopted legislation, the antimonopoly institutions of the Union and republics should decide to disband the production associations and enterprises that may be considered monopolies, and set up ways to control the activity of enterprises whose technology controls the activity in a technologically monopolistic enterprise.

During this stage most of the work to create competitive conditions among the domestic manufacturers should be carried out to the extent that it does not cause large structural reorganization of production. The scope for such reorganization will be limited by reduced investment under conditions of rigid financial and credit limitations.

At this time in the economy a contradictory process will take place. On the one hand, one may expect that more and more goods will be available in the market. A market infrastructure will be developing at a rapid pace; private business activity will strengthen its influence on the economy. The utilization of material resources should be more efficient, the production inventory will be reduced. The resources released in this way will be directed to the market for the means of production, thus facilitating its stabilization.

On the other hand, one may expect the crisis to deepen because of the dismantling of the administrative-command system, price instability, reorganization of economic relations and financial-credit policy. Due to reduction of investment activity, one may expect a decline in production, particularly in such basic branches as construction and machine building. The above phenomenon cannot be considered as negative since it will mark the start of structural shifts in the national economy where an unduly large share of the support was allocated to inefficient production in these branches. More efficient utilization of resources will reduce the demand for intermediate products.

At the same time, it will cause a worsening of the financial situation and may lead to the bankruptcy of some enterprises. The problem of unemployment will become acute, particularly in the regions where enterprises of extractive heavy industry are located. The appropriate institutions should support the employees of such enterprises, ensuring employment for them, retraining them, and rendering them any kind of assistance to enable them to adapt to new conditions. These institutions should not assist those enterprises that manufacture unnecessary products and swallow up valuable material resources.

Within this period the pressure on state institutions dealing with the problems of employment and public works programs (which are to be developed beginning in the first stage) will be considerably strengthened.

Support for small private business should help to increase the number of jobs.

But an alternative course of events could be envisaged. If a rigid financial-credit policy is not pursued, inflationary pressures will strengthen because the market situation will favor a rise in prices for consumer goods, which will increase demands for wage growth.

Competition and private business, if not properly developed at this moment, will not be in a position to stabilize the market.

Under such conditions a stabilizing factor could be the rapid development of the housing market and housing reform as well as wage reform; the changing of relations between enterprises and local soviets will help solve the problems of completion, price liberalization, and internal ruble convertibility.

The housing market should be regarded as an integral part of the process of transition to a market economy. It may help to absorb a large part of the excess liquidity of the population, rebalancing the consumer market on a long-term basis and strengthening the stimuli for labor activity.

The wage system also should be reconsidered, including state regulation of the minimum wage for enterprises under all forms of ownership. The state minimum wage should be calculated on the basis of the minimum household budget, taking into account the new level of expenses for living accommodations and the broader range of goods and services to be obtained at market prices out of personal income. The minimum wage will be a very important social benefit.

In connection with the above measures, the republics and local authorities are to intensify their efforts to remove from enterprises the excessive and unevenly distributed burden arising from their responsibility for social security. The primary expenditure for these purposes, particularly for housing construction and maintenance of living accommodations and facilities, should be undertaken by the local soviets. An appropriate provision should be prepared for these purposes. These measures will facilitate the transition of enterprises to market relations and increase their capacity to compete in the market.

In connection with the above measures reforms should be completed in the formation of prices. By the end of 400 days state control over prices should be removed from approximately 70 to 80 percent of goods and services. It should mainly be retained for primary resources (i.e., crude oil, petroleum products, gas, and some kinds of ferrous and nonferrous metals), a limited quantity of basic consumer goods (some kinds of bread, meat, milk, sugar, vegetable oil, over-the-counter medicine, school textbooks, fares for public transport, and utility tariffs). With prices determined predominantly by the equilibrium of supply and demand and a properly balanced budget, the key problem of the transition to a market economy will be the internal convertibility of the ruble. This lies at the heart of ensuring that all domestic enterprises and foreign companies on the territory of the USSR are free to buy and sell the currency required for transactions according to the market rate of exchange.

Internal convertibility of the ruble will facilitate a sizable influx of foreign investment, which is urgently required for the country to effect structural reorganization and technical reequipment, as well as to develop competition in the internal market and to overcome monopoly. One may assert that under the conditions in our country this may be considered as a decisive prerequisite for the next stage of putting the market mechanism into full operation. Important steps to make the ruble convertible will be taken even in the first stage of the reform, within the first 100 days. But at this stage convertibility will be limited, both with respect to the transactions as well as with respect to the category of buyers. This may be explained by the fact that fixed state prices will be kept for most goods; only the first steps of a currency market will be undertaken during this stage.

The introduction of ruble convertibility involves:

- the development of a currency market (currency auctions, stock exchanges, and allowing commercial banks to undertake currency transactions);
- the introduction and adjustment of new customs tariffs, export fees, and charges to ensure that internal prices correspond approximately to world prices (thus preempting possible black market activity).

These measures would considerably reduce the volume of quotas and licenses.

THE 400TH TO 500TH DAYS: BEGINNING OF THE UPSWING

The main task of this stage is to consolidate the stabilization of the economy and of finances to prompt the creation of a self-regulating competitive market.

The central feature of this period will be the considerable progress in denationalizing, privatizing, and demonopolizing the economy, and activating a policy of industrial restructuring.

Prerequisites for a tangible strengthening of economic activity should occur first in light industry and the food industry, in the agricultural sector and in services. Should the measures specified for the first 400 days prove successful, the national economy will undergo a radical change. Before the beginning of the last stage practically all the main conditions for a stable, functioning economy will be created, namely: equilibrium of prices and a balanced budget, a modernized banking system and a currency market.

Denationalization and privatization will accelerate. Before the 500th day not less than 70 percent of industrial enterprises, 30 to 90 percent of construction projects, vehicular transportation services, wholesale trade in intermediate products, retail trade, public food supply, and services should be transformed into joint-stock companies, sold or leased.

The funds and committees dealing with state property will transfer the shares belonging to the state to physical and legal persons either directly or through appropriate companies.

Republican and local authorities will carry out the antimonopoly program, i.e., support for small enterprises will be strengthened, and unprofitable enterprises will be separated as independent enterprises and be developed. Foreign competitors will start to operate on the internal market. Domestic manufacturers will be protected by customs tariffs.

Housing reform will help to raise labor mobility. The system of passport registration will be abolished. Appropriate alterations will be introduced into labor legislation. It is necessary to create and strengthen independent trade unions as future defenders of the interests of workers, entrepreneurs and managers. On the basis of agreements reached among them, and with the regulating role of the state, it will be possible to create a labor market and establish public control over incomes and prices.

The development of financial markets requires the introduction of taxes on capital.

The development of competition, private business, and price stabilization will be accompanied by a decline in the number of financial reorganizations. The envisaged reduction of income taxes will stimulate business activity.

A reduction of interest rates and reserve requirements of the Reserve System of the Union is also contemplated. This will allow for increased investment.

A large-scale restructuring of the economy will be undertaken according to market mechanisms and will attract investment, technology, and managerial experience. This reorganization will take a long time, but before there is complete fulfillment of the program, a real restructuring of the economy will have been undertaken.

As a result of implementing all these measures within a short time, the basis of a new economic system will be established. This system will orient production toward satisfaction of personal and collective needs, create effective stimuli for work and private business, ensure adequate satiation of market demand for a wide variety of goods at stable prices, and lay the foundation for the country's prosperity as well as that of all people living there.

The sections following will provide a fuller description of the measures to be taken in respective areas of the program.

5

Mechanisms for Maintaining Stability in Production During the Transition Period

IMMEDIATE MEASURES

At the present time breaking apart the economic ties that had formed in the past has proven to be very dangerous; even now it affects production. The collapse of the monetary system and the drop in the ruble's purchasing power has resulted in a system of bartering and the economic isolation of the republics and regions which are determined to settle independently their problems of shortages of material resources and goods. This situation introduces confusion into the national economy, disorganizes economic relations, extremely complicates the supply of materials and machinery, and may cause an economically unjustified drop in production.

In the framework of the existing system much work is devoted to determining the magnitude and composition of state contracts and providing them with the material resources, to coordinating the plans of the enterprises, and to concluding these agreements for 1991. To a considerable extent this work is disorganized due to the lack of any decision on price reform and the revision of economic ties.

Reorganization of the system of economic ties is urgently required because the system has proven to be inefficient and irrational. But as experience shows, spontaneous reorganization is very painful and accompanied by large losses.

To keep the stability of production the group of measures previously discussed in the section entitled "100 Days" should be taken.

STATE ORDERS AND PRICES

In the transition period, government contracts shall be preserved in their role as the instrument of direct state economic regulation. But their terms and conditions of placement will undergo considerable change.

Government contracts will regain their true purpose; they shall be concluded in the form of agreements. The contractual form permits enterprises of any form of incorporation to avoid an unprofitable government contract. Beginning in 1991 all government contracts shall be concluded by the appropriate bodies of the State Contract System. Thus, there will be two types of contracts: on the one hand contracts between the SCS, acting on behalf of the government, and manufacturers, and on the other hand contracts between manufacturers and their customers.

The list of goods and the volume of shipments, the recipients of the shipments, the mutual obligations of the parties and sanctions for unfulfilled obligations, as well as the negotiated prices and terms of trade, and the circumstance for changing prices over the course of the agreement all will be stipulated in the general agreement.

During the transition period all government contracts will remain obligatory and any case of refusal to conclude a shipment agreement will be sanctioned accordingly.

The profitability of government contracts for the manufacturer will be ensured by:

- negotiated price;
- state allocation of material resources mentioned in the government contract, with deductions from taxes on profits in the range of 1.5 to 2 percent of the cost of the product to be produced under the state contract.

Determining the deductions on a basis of total product value implies a very simple calculation and will considerably increase the profit that will remain fully disposable by the enterprises.

The volume and composition of state orders for defense production suppliers, for nonproductive organizations for special Union-level users, for export (under international agreements), and for commodity reserves, all will be defined at the Union level. Besides, the relevant Union bodies that represent all the republics will conclude multilateral agreements on reciprocal shipments of basic products (such as fuel, raw materials, industrial commodities, and consumer goods) and establish prices at which these shipments will be effected.

The volume and composition of government contracts agreed at the Union level shall then be transacted at the level of the republican contract systems. At this level government contracts take their final shape: they are adjusted with respect to the interrepublican agreements and the internal requirements of the enterprises for products which were not satisfied through purchases on the free market.

Setting government contract prices is of special importance. The present system of prices and adjustment coefficients is distorted; therefore starting from 1991 we suggest switching to wholesale price contracts. Fixed state prices shall be retained only for fuel, power resources, raw materials, and some other products determined by interrepublic agreements.

The contract prices, as well as the conditions of their adjustment, will be approved by the State Contract System bodies that sign the government contracts after negotiations with manufacturers, major customers, and wholesale enterprises; such agreements will take into account costs, fixed prices, and the level of market prices, if they are known. The introduction of this procedure of setting wholesale contract prices in the course of the allocation of government contracts is a very important step in price reform. These government contracts and prices can be used to regulate the markets for the means of production, agricultural products, and consumer goods.

THE STATE CONTRACT SYSTEM

The bodies of the State Contract System will be responsible for allocating government contracts and the output produced under these negotiated contract prices, signing appropriate general agreements. Such a State Contract System will be created in the autumn of 1990, at the level of the Union republics and the Union of the SSR from the administrative organs of Gossnab, Mintorg, and Agrosnab.

During the transition period this system shall have the authority to act as state intermediary.

The State Contract organs will be separated from commercial wholesale enterprises that will act independently. Relationships between these enterprises will be formed on a commercial basis.

The State Contract System will include regional organs with commodity divisions which will allocate government contracts and products, and divisions that will coordinate activities for the material support of the government contracts.

The volume and composition of government contracts will be fixed by the republican and Union contract system bodies.

The following organizational structure of the State Contract System bodies is proposed:

Enterprises, with the help of wholesale dealers, independently form a portfolio of orders, plan production, distribute orders, and sign contracts. If it turns out that it is impossible to order some products or that a plant cannot reach its full production capacity (i.e., if market relations do not work), they will notify the territorial state contract organs, and provide them with the necessary information.

Thus, the State Contract System operates on the principle of exceptions without hindering the development of market ties, and with the help of information provided about idle capacity, the republican bodies determine the magnitude and composition of government contracts, and the requirements of the republics for reciprocal shipments. On the basis of these requirements, bilateral and multilateral interrepublican agreements will be drafted.

On this basis the republican and territorial bodies distribute contracts, negotiate prices, and allocate material resources. They communicate with producers, major customers, and wholesale intermediaries, who represent the interests of small consumers. The volume of government contracts should be as small as possible so as not to hinder the development of market relations.

For 1991 the State Contract System bodies shall, in special cases, be granted a right to terminate or suspend contracts previously concluded between enterprises if state interests dictate the necessity to reorient the existing commodity flows.

To prevent arbitrary decisions of this nature, enterprises are given the right to contest a decision by arbitration, which can either repeal the decision of the Contract System bodies or recover damages caused to the enterprise by any unjustified decisions.

The State Contract System may be used to exercise control over monopolistic producers by regulating prices for their products and enforcing the integrity of consumers.

THE CONSUMER MARKET

The sphere most sensitive to unstable supplies, and which therefore badly needs special measures for their prevention during the transition period, is the consumer market.

Eventual liberalization of prices for consumer goods and services may lead to a situation in which some groups of the population might be deprived of the possibility to purchase basic necessities. Such a situation will call for appropriate steps from the republican and local authorities.

In view of the above it is necessary to act according to the following guidelines:

1. Accelerated demonopolization and privatization of the retail and wholesale trade, the public consumer services, and a considerable part of the enterprises which deliver goods to them. Trade has the greatest number of small enterprises, but here monopolization is of an explicitly organizational nature. It creates the most favorable conditions for the activities of the shadow economy.

   The current middle-level administrative structures which carry out bookkeeping, accounting, and planning within their framework are subject to reorganization or liquidation, taking due account of the requirements of antimonopoly legislation.

2. Mobilization of commodity reserves and creation of conditions for regulation of the consumer market through "commodity interventions."

   For nonfood goods, and also for a number of foodstuffs, it is possible during the four to five months preceding the liberalization of prices for these goods to reserve from 3 to 7 percent of the goods turnover.

   Reserves may be accumulated from the reduction of limited-access sales and other forms of distribution of nonfood consumer goods. In 1989 the following were sold through said channels: footwear - 11 percent; refrigerators - 14 percent; sewing machines - 71.5 percent; color TV sets - 10.5 percent; washing machines - 19 percent; furniture - 14 percent. During the remaining four months of 1990 considerable stocks can be accumulated on account of such sources.

   It is necessary to maximize the use of foreign aid for these purposes.

   Under present-day conditions concentration of reserves and conveyance of goods and their storage may require special channels and means. Peoples' deputies at all levels and representatives of workers' control might be involved in this work.

3. Use of the mechanisms of state contracts and prices and the contract system can ensure a certain production output and prevent a sizable reduction in production of consumer goods; in order to ensure an even distribution of commodities throughout the country, it is expedient to establish at the Union level of the state contract system the interrepublican commodity council, which will comprise the plenipotentiaries of the Union republics.

4. The introduction at the level of cities, regions, and republics of rationing, for certain everyday products, shall guarantee a minimum level of consumption.

    Of late the local authorities have accumulated sizable experience in this sphere. It seems that in addition to income indexation, in taking account of local conditions it will be necessary to use this accumulated experience to the considerable detriment of the population.

    We recommend that rationing be limited to only a narrow range of foodstuffs and other basic necessities at minimum rates in the event they are in short supply. This will allow the sale of remaining stock at market prices in the commercial trade network. In the event of rationing, fixed prices can be used, with subsidies from the local budget going to trade organizations. There is another more flexible option: the introduction of food rationing cards to be used for purchasing at discount prices. A 50 to 70 percent discount from the market price will be compensated through the local budget. To cover these expenses, the local authorities may introduce a tax on personal income, or use other sources. Food rationing cards will be given only to specific groups of the population.

5. Promotion of the activities of consumer cooperation, trading, and purchasing cooperatives engaged in the delivery and marketing of goods in the regions experiencing shortages.

All the above-mentioned measures would be of a temporary nature; they should be introduced for a limited period of time and repealed as soon as the market and prices become stabilized.

THE STABILIZATION FUNDS

During the transition period many enterprises will suffer serious financial difficulties as a result of austere monetary policy, including difficulties which are not of their own making, but which arise due to the irregular dynamics of prices and other reasons. It will take some time to adjust to conditions of financial austerity.

The difficulties connected therewith will be lifted by establishing special stabilization funds which will render temporary financial aid to enterprises in the form of direct subsidies, subsidized soft loans, credit guarantees, credit at low interest rates.

The resources for the stabilization funds at the level of the Union and the republics are formed from targeted budget allocation, bonds sales and earnings from lotteries.

The financial aid from the stabilization funds will be rendered in the event of certain predefined conditions. The funds will be entitled to consider only justified detailed requests from state enterprises which were actually affected by the new economic policy and can demand any information from the applicants. Assistance may be conditioned by reorganization of the enterprise, a change in management, the reduction of nonproduction costs or the number of personnel, sales of surplus stocks and equipment, changes in product mix, division of the enterprise into two or more enterprises, etc.

The funds will invite highly skilled experts who will analyze the operation of enterprises and prepare recommendations for the funds.

ACCELERATED DEVELOPMENT OF A MARKET INFRASTRUCTURE

The formation of a market infrastructure and across-the-board support of any initiative in this sphere should be considered as a priority task at all levels. The guidelines in this field are:

1. Development of a network of commercial wholesale establishments for marketing the means of production, agricultural products, and consumer goods. Denationalization and privatization of said establishments through leasing, sales of fixed production assets of current bodies of the State Committee of the USSR for Material and Technical Supplies, the Ministry of Trade of the USSR, the Committee for Agricultural Supplies and their transformation into joint-stock companies;

2. Encouragement of new trading-and-purchasing cooperatives, and any other enterprises in this sphere;

3. Establishment, by spring of 1991, of a network of commodities exchanges for wholesale trade in diversified groups of commodities together with the raw materials for their manufacture; approval of

regulations for the commodities exchanges. An increase in the number of trade fairs and changes in their work;

4. Encouragement of investments in the market infrastructure, the construction of depots and warehouses, a commercial information network, premises for exchanges and fairs. The transfer of available premises suitable for these purposes is of special importance for the development of a system of warehouses for agricultural products directed at producing farms.

NOTES FOR PART 1

1 The growth of ratio of money supply (M_3, cash and bank money) to GNP is an extreme symptom of the economic policy implemented these past years and a source of the present financial crisis. The chart shows how the growth of the money supply accelerated after 1987 (the M_3 decline in 1986 was connected with methodology changes).

2 The text of this chapter has been agreed verbatim (word by word) with representatives of the republics which took part in the elaboration of the program. It may differ in some points from stipulations contained in the program's other chapters.

3 In the interim period, any restrictions on free trade or exchange of major commodities shall be prohibited. The maximum prices and quantities of goods to be freely supplied to the All-Union market shall be defined by all republics in a separate agreement.

4 The bracketed inclusion was suggested by some of the republics.

PART II

THE BASIC BLOCKS OF THE TRANSITION PROGRAM

1

Denationalization and the Development of Competition

SUPPORT OF ENTREPRENEURSHIP

A most important task of the initial stage of the transition to a market economy is to create appropriate conditions for the development of the key figure of market relations: the entrepreneur. For many years, in our country, entrepreneurship was not appreciated, it was penalized. Now it is necessary to recognize that the only resource to be relied upon during transition to the market economy is the potential of human activity, motivated by people's desire to lead a normal life.

Joint-stock companies, leaseholders, private and public enterprises, should take part in market competition on equal terms. No ideological considerations can be placed above economic efficiency.

One of the major obstacles to formation of the market, and to development of competition and entrepreneurship, is an extremely high degree of monopolization in the Soviet economy that emerged as a result of the perennial policy of concentration and narrow specialization of production with the formation of hierarchical structures inherent to the administrative-command system. From here comes the extreme importance of demonopolization of the economy — the necessity to implement a wide-scale antimonopoly program.

The republics are to accept the entrepreneurship encouragement programs.

The first steps of these programs will be explicit legal guarantees for free entrepreneurship (guarantees against nationalization, expropriation, and discrimination). For this purpose a system of legal acts is to be passed which ensure the development of individual (private) entrepreneurship, joint-stock companies and cooperatives.

General guarantees are provided at the Union level (the decree of the USSR President "On Freedom and Protection of Entrepreneurship"). Specific legal acts will be passed at the level of the Union republics. The USSR President submits the appropriate amendments and additions to the constitution to the Congress of People's Deputies of the USSR.

At the very outset of implementation of the program, the Union republics, by mutual agreement, submit for approval by the USSR President lists of specific activities that are prohibited on the territory of the USSR or have the status of state monopolies or may be pursued only under state license. All other kinds are governed by the principle "All that is not prohibited is permitted."

By October 10 the supreme soviets of the Union republics will introduce the necessary amendments on civil procedures to the criminal and administrative codes to repeal all legal restrictions on entrepreneurship. Amnesty is declared for all those who are serving sentences under the criminal codes that are being abolished. New articles of the criminal codes which will reinforce the protection of property rights are to be adopted and quite possibly the republics will set up public funds to support these aims.

The republics introduce laws (regulations) describing the procedures for establishing enterprises and their status, including nonprofit enterprises; the procedures for starting new business activities, reorganization and bankruptcy; and responsibilities of the owners of enterprises. Amendments are to be introduced to the republican labor codes and other documents which will regulate the rules for private labor employment.

By November 1 the central banks of the republics will have approved the rules for crediting the initial operations of businesses, rules for mortgage operations by banks, and set forth the rules for crediting private individuals to promote the formation of new enterprises.

The republics adopt coordinated laws regarding the legal economic status of foreigners in the USSR and the protection of foreign investments on the territory of the USSR.

The notion of "higher authority" will no longer exist for state enterprises: they become independent business units and bear all responsibility for the results of their activities.

By early 1991, uniform rules conforming closely to the international standards for bookkeeping and accounting will be established for all enterprises. The form and procedure for the annual publication of balance sheets for all enterprises will be approved, thus allowing glasnost to spread to these activities.

All this will permit us to create the basis for developing entrepreneurship, which will become the mainstay for the entire economic reform.

DENATIONALIZATION

Denationalization should be comprehensive in nature and it should cover simultaneously large-scale industry, small and medium enterprises in trade, industry, and services, housing and residential construction, land-tenure reform (see the corresponding sections). The laws which regulate property relations should be of universal character.

From the first day after approval of the program for transition to a market economy, denationalization and privatization of property will spread widely along the following main principles:

- participation of the working people at large;
- separation of management and ownership;
- paying for property;
- a wide range of methods and approaches, including regional ones;
- aiming at the liquidation of monopolies;
- priority to enterprises which seize the initiative in privatization.

The main task of the preparatory stage (up to October 1, 1990) is to shape a clear-cut and efficient program of privatization and adoption of a package of laws on denationalization. This package should include the laws which regulate the denationalization process and ensure the autonomy of small firms in all spheres of the economy and the freedom of newly established structures — such as joint-stock companies — from official control at all levels.

The elaboration of guidelines for breaking up industrial enterprises and an antimonopoly policy in trade and services will be completed during this period. The principles of support for competition will be set up. Audit firms, commodity and securities exchange supervisory bodies, agencies to control prices and taxes, arbitration and/or arbitrage (economic) courts will be set up.

One of the main criteria of the quality of the legal and constitutional provisions for the reform is their compatibility with international standards.

Denationalization is conducted under the guidance of committees for administering the state property of the republics, the State Property Fund of the USSR (SPF), and local government bodies.

The difference in local conditions will be reflected in specific forms, methods, and scales of privatization in each republic, but the general basic principles of denationalization will be preserved.

During the first month of the reform (by October 15) the republican governments and the SPF together will make decisions on the delimitation of powers to denationalize enterprises, implying not a division of property, but the sharing of responsibility to conduct the operation.

Only a very limited number of enterprises and firms need to remain directly responsible to Union administrative agencies: defense enterprises that are outside of the conversion program; enterprises using nuclear technologies; pipelines; long-distance communication networks; KGB and Defense Ministry military installations; major railways and some others. During the next few years the postal service, telegraph, and the energy system will also remain under direct state control. The status of such enterprises has to be approved before January 1, 1991, and they are to make contracts with republican and local government bodies to secure their rights to use resources (land and water) according to the state of affairs on that date.

Denationalization of major enterprises at the Union level will be organized in such industries as aerospace and communications equipment facilities, electronics, shipbuilding, the merchant marine fleet, seaports with All-Union status, and some others. The prevailing form for such enterprises will be the transrepublican joint-stock company, with share distribution among the republican committees administering state property. The list of enterprises to be transformed into transrepublican companies and the principles for the share distribution will be coordinated with all the Union republics.

Delimitation of powers between republican and local bodies to denationalize other property on the territories of the republics will evidently be left for the republics to decide. Local governmental bodies will conduct denationalization and privatization in such spheres as trade, services, cafes and restaurants, agriculture, public utilities, motor vehicle transportation, and small industrial enterprises.

By November 1, the SPF, the republican committees administering state property, and the local soviets are to publish lists of enterprises to be denationalized (in accordance with the decision for the delimitation of powers). Collectives of workers of those enterprises will be given a month to propose specific forms of denationalization (leasing, buying-out of collective property, transformation into cooperatives, etc.) for consideration by the appropriate bodies. Afterward the right to decide about forms of denationalization will belong to the state as the owner of the property at the time of the beginning of the reform.

In conducting denationalization, priority will be given to construction and production of materials for construction, motor vehicle transportation, services, cafes and restaurants, consumer goods and food industries, material supply, and wholesale trade organizations. In these spheres denationalization is to be finished in the shortest possible time.

The rates and forms of privatizing small local enterprises of different industries are to be determined locally. The basic form of denationalizing such enterprises is to sell them to private individuals or groups at auctions (allowing for payment in installments); they are to be transformed later into firms or partnerships. Another possibility should not be excluded, that is, leasing them to private persons or work collectives on the understanding that they are to buy them out in the future.

Auctions must be held openly, so as to attract public attention and ensure financial and public control of denationalization. To ensure the success of such auctions, republican committees administering state property are to approve, by October 15, the basic rules on auction sales, the methods of assessing enterprises, and the rules of purchase and lease.

In the retail foodstuffs trade, it seems reasonable to sell small stores with floor area under 100 square meters and staff under seven to private owners. That means that 68 percent of the food stores, with 30 percent of the turnover of these goods, and with 500,000 employees, will leave the state sector. At least half of this is to be accomplished by the spring of 1991.

The remaining state-owned stores are to be transferred into joint-stock companies, cooperatives, or collectively owned companies.

In the nonfood retail trade, privatization will apply to stores with floor area under 160 square meters and up to 10 employees. Seventy-seven thousand stores with 700,000 employees that sell approximately 30 percent of consumer goods will become private property. Denationalization of these enterprises must start in the current year.

By the end of 1991 the state will be controlling only that part of the retail trade which will distribute some rationed basic goods. Large stores may remain as communal property operating as malls and leasing their space to various users including industrial firms, cooperatives, and foreign firms.

Wholesale trade enterprises with their storehouses and depots are to be denationalized as well. Measures must be envisaged to prevent them from monopolizing wholesale trade flows.

Concurrent with denationalization of trade must be measures to liberalize pricing and denationalize manufacturing enterprises to prevent the stifling of market-type trade by state-sector enterprises and bureaucracy.

In the food industry, the first to be sold will be small cafes and restaurants that serve under 50 customers simultaneously and have under five employees on average. That covers approximately 50,000 enterprises with up to 60 percent of all customers served, and up to 60 percent of sales.

The major part of small-scale property is to be denationalized during the first 500 days. If successfully organized, this process can lead to 20 percent of enterprises leaving the state sector by the end of 1990, 60 to 70 percent by the middle of 1991, and 80 percent by the end of 1991. In other words, the process of denationalization may be considered finished by that time.

Experience shows that the most effective form of denationalization of large state-owned enterprises is establishing independent joint-stock societies, which leads to a sharp increase in responsibility for decision-making, especially for financial decisions.

At the same time it takes more time, personnel, organization, and coordination effort to establish a system of large modern joint-stock societies, as this process must be coordinated with reorganizing the system (and structure) of people's savings, major changes in the financial system, gradual formation of securities markets and large foreign investments.

This includes:

- setting up groups of experts to transform individual enterprises;
- assessment of property: balance-sheet values, properly adjusted for various factors (including location);
- assessment of building and equipment (age, wear, foreign origin, prospect to modernize for rubles, prospect for upgrading technologies); market value of trademarks, R&D potential, product competitiveness under conditions of broader imports;
- economic analysis: possible need to break the enterprise into several smaller ones; what assets, excessive inventories, and equipment can be appropriated by the state and sold later;
- market research: competitors inside the country, the positions of suppliers and consumers, the prospects for sales, the dynamics of prices of manufactured goods, and the factors for production and exporting potential;
- preparing a draft of the charter of the society, determining equity capital and other specific criteria;

DENATIONALIZATION OF INDUSTRY

(potential dynamics of the process is in the next 7–12 years)

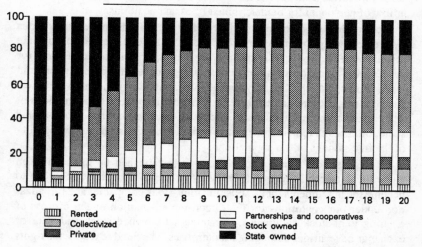

Legend	
▦ Rented	☐ Partnerships and cooperatives
▨ Collectivized	▨ Stock owned
■ Private	■ State owned

- determining the structure of the firm, its reorganization (breaking it into smaller ones and restructuring of funds); determining the internal managerial structure (separation of powers and responsibilities of the management and the board of directors);
- determining the structure of ownership (collective of workers, foreign investors, administration, distribution of shares among institutional investors, determining what part of stock can be sold to the public) and search for potential funders and investors;
- search for resources to compensate unneeded employees, drafting plans for job placement of unneeded employees and early retirement;
- coordination with the SPF and control bodies (SEC equivalent and others) of the proposed form of privatization and stock issuance, determination of a time schedule and specific stages;
- registration of potential investors;
- determining market prices of the stock and the system of selling it; and
- the sale of stock.

Even with the shortest possible terms for all these stages and the involvement of all experts in the country, fast transformation of the majority of industrial enterprises into joint-stock companies is impossible. For these purposes personnel need to be trained, both inside the country, and also abroad. Starting in the fall of 1990, capable people must be sent to be trained abroad for terms from several months to several years so as to have a regular inflow of personnel for predetermined roles and positions.

At the first stage of the project a few dozen enterprises in various industries may be thus transformed in order to gain experience, improve the organization of production, and prepare the constitutional documents for these various industries (mining, consumer goods and food, machinery and tools, and publishing). It is at this stage that republics will develop their own approaches to denationalization. The selection of the forms and methods of denationalization (from issuing stock to privatization) is related to the sociopolitical situation in the country, national traditions, and the availability of the free savings of the population.

The Investment Funds ("Funds"), to be established by the republican committees administering state property or the SPF of the USSR, are to become the instruments for establishing joint-stock companies and privatization under our conditions for the direct implementation of the process of creating joint-stock companies, managing state-owned stock and sales or exchange of securities belonging to enterprises. The Funds exercise the rights of controlling-interest holders but do not interfere with the day-to-day operation of the enterprises. The Funds are formed on the basis of industrial, territorial, or any other principle accepted by the committee.

During the 1991-1992 period the funds will organize stock companies on the basis of enterprises and later, depending on their charter, will have the right to sell or transfer to other owners up to 100 percent of the stock of the enterprise in question. Each Fund will develop a medium-term plan for selling shares, to be approved by the committee. Even during the first 500 days the maximum possible amount of shares will be sold to enterprises and individuals. The advantage of this operation is its speed, and the disadvantage is that it will be impossible to determine in a short period the true (market) value of stocks being sold.

Given the undeveloped financial system of the country, the Investment Funds would facilitate the exchange of stock between enterprises, banks and other funds. After some time, the Funds will be transformed into financial institutions of a different type (investment banks, finance companies, etc.) and control large stock portfolios. In effect, the Funds will be the holders of republican stock in transrepublican companies.

Shares can be sold on conditions of payment in installments, or using credit or credit guarantees of the Investment Funds and banks involved in the process of privatization. Some capital stock items or shares can change hands without payment, or with deferred payment at a specified price. In cases when no one is willing to buy shares in a particular firm or accept them as a result of an exchange, it would be possible to hand them over to a manager or a group of managers who are given a free hand for an unspecified period, along the same lines as leasing to collectives of workers (with the right to buy out the firm in the future).

Money received after selling stock and part of the resources of enterprises will go to the committee administering state property or its subsidiary funds and be used to repay debts and provide severance pay for unneeded employees. All or part of the funds can accumulate financial resources and later be transformed into investment banks.

From the start special attention will be attached to attracting foreign capital to privatization (direct sales of stock and offers of stock as debt repayment).

FINANCIAL ASPECTS OF DENATIONALIZATION

Of independent significance is the participation of the workers' collectives in buying stock. The enterprises are property that belongs to the entire society, and the rights of their employees are important though not prevailing. At the same time as far as labor relations are concerned, the involvement of workers' collectives in management is envisioned by all forms of legislation regulating enterprises. The Funds can leave up to 10 percent of the shares for the enterprises so that they may sell them or hand them out to employees on favorable terms so as to make them shareholders with full rights. It may become reasonable or even necessary to exchange the shares held by the workers' collectives for shares that will give its members full voting rights.

The existing accounting data consists of assets which, even if corrected to account for depreciation, do not reflect market evaluation of the costs of an enterprise. Uncertainty will initially pull down stock prices. This will stimulate the purchase of property and securities but decrease the proceeds from sale.

Overall there are potentially up to 46,000 industrial and 760,000 trade enterprises in the country to be denationalized or privatized. By early 1990 the accumulated stock of fixed capital in the USSR was almost 3 trillion rubles, approximately 2 trillion in industries (approximately 850 billion in manufacturing).

Even allowing for wear and tear (33 percent average, 45 percent in industry) and generally low efficiency, it is a huge sum — 1959 billion rubles in the entire country, including 469 billion rubles in industry. It amounts to seven thousand rubles per capita, or three times the average per capita gross income. Forty-five percent of capital is concentrated in industry, 19.6 percent in agriculture, 17.9 percent in transport and 4.5 percent in construction.

The potential demand of the general public for property is evaluated by type of property, such as housing, land, productive assets of small businesses in various branches of the economy, stocks of newly established companies, and government bonds. In 1991-1992 total investment by the population can be expected to amount to 50-60 billion a year.

Funds received from selling stocks by republican committees administering state property, minus the costs and those funds that they keep, will be withdrawn from circulation (eliminated). Up to 10 percent of funds received by local soviets from the selling-off of enterprises will be directed to local budgets, while the rest is to be withdrawn from circulation.

OVERCOMING MONOPOLISM

One of the most important tasks of government regulation of the economy is to contain monopolistic practices.

According to the USSR State Committee for Supplies (Gossnab), almost two thousand products with a total value of 11 billion rubles are manufactured by only one enterprise. The share of monopoly-manufactured products in the machinery industry is 80 percent of the entire production. According to data from the State Committee for Statistics, there are 166 monopoly enterprises and 180 monopoly producers in machinery alone: in 209 out of 304 broad groups based on certain products. In specific products the level of monopolization is even higher than in the broad product groups. For example, 96 percent of diesel locomotives are manufactured by the Voroshilovogradteplovoz, 100 percent of air conditioning machines for homes and offices are manufactured by the consortium Bakkonditsioner, 100 percent of deep-water pumps are manufactured by the Dzerzhinsky factory in Baku, etc.

New organizational structures — concerns, interindustrial state corporations (ISC's), associations, consortiums, etc. are often formed as monopolies. For example, the association Agrockhim (former Ministry for Fertilizer Production) is a pure monopoly. Energomash ISC and QuanTEMP ISC account for one-half and two-thirds respectively of the total production of hydraulic and steam turbines, galvanic elements and batteries.

Distribution of resources through monopoly-type central agencies, above all the USSR State Planning Committee (Gosplan) and USSR State Committee for Supplies (Gossnab). The Ministry of Trade of the USSR, Centrosoyuz, is the most powerful brake on the major holder of resources. It controls almost 60 percent of centralized distribution of products (ministries and agencies control approximately 30 percent, and the State Committee for Supplies controls more than 10 percent). This unnecessary centralization of supplies and sales of products is characteristic of all leading branches of the economy.

An antimonopoly program is supposed to promote competition and market relations and will comprise the following major directions:

1. The complete elimination of the administrative-command system, and those elements of the system that contribute to preservation and reproduction of monopolistic relations;
2. introduction of changes in the structure of production, the breaking-up and diversification of existing enterprises;
3. creation of organizational and legal mechanisms to pinpoint and overcome the manifestations of monopoly in the economy.

The success of the antimonopoly measures will depend largely on the formation of a market infrastructure. It will be closely linked to such processes as improving the monetary and financial system, enlisting a new system of price formation, pricing liberalization, and forming a financial market. The implementation of the entire package of antimonopoly measures should be launched as the very first steps of the program for reform.

It will be especially important to agree that the republics all take a uniform approach to ensure the stable operation of market mechanisms. Union and republican antimonopoly committees need to be established in September 1990 to conduct a coordinated struggle with the monopolies. The Union committee will be formed on the basis of federated principles, will be comprised of representatives of all the republics, and will regulate the All-Union market.

Support from the republics should take the form of legislation along similar lines. The law laying the foundation for antimonopoly legislation in the USSR as basic legislation and the corresponding legislative acts of the republics must be adopted before January 1, 1991. These results are expected: to define the fundamental rules for the agencies involved with economic mechanisms and for the organs of state power and control; to establish criteria to identify unfair competition and monopoly-type activities, such as the limitation or interruption of the production of goods that are in short supply, refusal to make contracts despite the potential for production, imposing conditions on contracts that are not related to the subject matter, and imposing a choice of goods; and to determine cases of illegal agreements used to divide the market and limit access to other producers.

Before the middle of 1991 the absolute monopoly in trade and the system of distribution of goods should be broken up. It should be replaced by horizontal market-type structures with a sufficient number of producers and consumers to ensure choice and competition.

To replace such monopolies as the Ministry of Trade and Centrosoyuz, various trade organizations that have been formed in the republics should be encouraged: retail partnerships, commercial associations, joint-stock companies, trade and middlemen cooperatives, and stores. The currently operating trade authorities, which in their majority are administrative superstructures over trade, should be eliminated.

Republican and local bodies of power should encourage the formation of active wholesale organizations, commercial banks, storehouses, packaging and transportation centers, information systems, and the other elements of a market infrastructure.

Implementation of the proposed measures will create the conditions needed to replace the vertical economic relations by horizontal ones, and that is a basic condition for creating a market, real decentralization, and eventual demonopolization of management.

At the start of the process of forming joint-stock companies from major state-owned enterprises and consortiums, the SPF of the USSR, the republican committees administering state property, and antimonopoly organizations should review each individual case and decide whether it makes sense to maintain it as a whole, or to divide it when there is need to do so, and withdraw and spinoff those structures that do not relate closely to the main product lines.

Justification of purely administrative methods of eliminating and splitting up enterprises should be substantiated by feasibility studies. Factors like the large expenditures tied to technology could work against forced division. In particular this applies to products that are unique or manufactured in small quantities, or mass-produced goods for limited application.

In such cases and also for major monopolies producing unique products, special pricing regimes are to be established (and coordinated with state organizations); they may be forced to sell a part of their products in foreign markets, and sell them to middlemen rather than directly to customers, etc.

Before the end of 1990 a list must be completed of functions that are forbidden to be concentrated in any type of company or partnership of companies. It must also be reflected in the antimonopoly legislation. This will serve as a basis on which to reconsider the constitutional documents of all organized groups of enterprises (associations, interindustrial state partnerships, consortiums, and concerns). If their structure does not conform to the legislation, they should be forcibly disbanded.

The attempts to weaken "natural" monopolies in such industries that cater to the entire state (such as transport, communications, pipelines) will meet with major difficulties. Effective measures will have to be worked out to weaken such monopolies as the Ministry of Railway Transport, the Ministry of Power Production, the Ministry of Sea Fleets, and the Ministry of Communications (Gasprom).

On the basis of foreign experience, parallel production will have to be started by firms that at first may be quite small but capable of competition. "Natural" monopolies will be placed under strict state control, especially their prices and the quality of their goods and services. Tougher than usual regulatory measures will be needed: obligatory state production targets, regulation of prices and tariffs.

One of the more efficient ways to overcome monopolies is to find an optimal balance of large, medium, and small firms. Judging by the experience of the development of cooperatives, fast changes can be expected here. Over the last two years the number of cooperatives has reached 200,000 producing 40 billion rubles' worth of goods annually.

Decisions have already been made at the Union level to encourage small firms. Their activities will follow the same rules as others. Their establishment procedure will be simplified. Tax incentives have to be introduced for the first two years of their activities. To develop small businesses, forcible and voluntary breakup of large monopolies is proposed, with the splitting off of their smaller constituents, if they can operate independently, to be established as firms, cooperatives, or leased enterprises, or the creation of branches on the initiative of associations and factories.

Small business needs support from the state. Specifically, small firms can be allowed to compete for pieces of land, unfinished or unused buildings, unused equipment and assets of bankrupt firms.

2

Finance and Credit Policies

A sound ruble will be the foundation for the acceleration of reform. Without a stable currency it is impossible to stabilize the economic structure, to have any order in the economy, to bring goods to market, and to move toward the new role of the state in the economy, toward more efficient production and integration into the global economy. It can be stated definitely that any extraordinary measures can only do harm without a resolution of the monetary issues.

THE BANKING SYSTEM

The main prerequisites for the success of reform are a unified monetary system and the preservation of a centralized monetary policy. This means that the State Bank system needs to be transformed in October, 1990, into a Union Reserve System as a voluntary union of central banks of the republics. The Union Reserve will have a board of governors with a chairman appointed by the President of the USSR and the central bank members of the system.

The board will make all important decisions by a qualified majority on votes on the issues of the monetary and credit policies to be implemented by the central republican banks. The Union Reserve will have no balance sheet of its own, but will prepare a balance sheet of the entire Union Reserve System. Republican banks will delegate specific functions to the Union Reserve, including the establishment and maintenance of the ruble exchange rates and the administration of the hard currency reserves of the Union.

The Union Reserve of the USSR will be a single judicial person; in other words, the monopoly on issuing cash and uniform principles of control will be preserved, even though republican banks will be responsible for actual cash emission, operating under the same rules as those for supervising commercial banks in the territory of their republics.

The republics will adopt laws on banking, if they do not conflict with the agreement which the Union Reserve has concluded, on condition that they shall not take unilateral measures to regulate or limit cash circulation or credit.

The central republican banks will be withdrawn from the control of republican governments and report annually to their respective supreme soviets, the latter having no right to interfere with the banks' day-to-day operations. For the duration of the transition period (until 1992) the Union Reserve and the central republican banks will cooperate closely with the organizations responsible for reform.

The key issue in the reform of the credit system is to commercialize the specialized state banks. They will be transformed into independent joint-stock companies with the broadest possible circulation of stock. The existing structures will not be ripped apart, but a partial separation of the specialized banks into regional and local commercial banks is a possibility.

The Vnesheconombank and the Savings Bank of the USSR will also be transformed along the same lines, but in their case demonopolization must be revealed above all in the elimination of their exclusive rights for foreign currency operations and for people's savings. Savings banks at all levels will be released from the control of the State Bank, new savings will no longer be removed automatically to the budget, and they will be able to develop as normal commercial banks.

Commercializing the banks means they will have to deal with those resources they have or can obtain, with independence in choosing where to place loans, and in establishing the price for loans and their terms. There will be uniform taxation and regulation for all banks, and clients will have the freedom to select banks. In September-October 1990 the banks should start operating on commercial principles, and the All-Union fund of loans should be divided up during the same period.

The system of universal commercial banks will be supplemented by specialized institutions — credit and loan cooperatives, investment and pension funds, and brokerage and leasing firms. To accomplish this, the central republican banks will issue regulatory documents on the basis of recommendations by the board of governors of the Union Reserve before the end of 1990 to legalize and create incentives for such activities.

The State Insurance System will be reorganized over the course of several months. The establishment of new insurance companies will be allowed, including those that have foreign partners. A system of state supervision of insurance will be set up. The resources of the insurance companies will no longer be turned over to the state treasury.

To provide financing and loans out of the state budget in 1991, governmental banks for development will be established to deal with large-scale investment projects.

State regulation of banking will amount to activities aimed at protecting the interests of clients. The central republican banks will be responsible for registering newly opened banks, overseeing their operations, and creating mechanisms to protect depositors' interests on the basis of contributions from the banks.

In October, interbank settlements will be restructured and banks will switch to correspondent relations. This will slow down interbranch operations and freeze large sums for a certain period. Central republican banks will provide clearing operations between banks to speed up operations at their level and will finalize agreements on a uniform system in the framework of the Union Reserve.

MONETARY AND CREDIT POLICIES

Under conditions of transition to a market-oriented economy, monetary policies will assume fundamentally new features. To assume control over monetary circulation and loans, a transition from loan and cash planning to regulation of the quantity of money will be accomplished starting in November. The key task for the initial months is a sharp limitation of loans and a decrease in the growth of the monetary aggregates.

Money supply definitions and relevant aggregates are under development. A system of collecting information and statistics is being developed. The task for 1990-1991 is to achieve zero growth of M_3. This can be achieved mainly via restriction of volume and consequently of deposits of enterprises. Deposits of the population will decrease if the program of tying up real cash prevails over the growth of personal incomes.

The instruments for regulation are:

- reserve requirements — the part of a bank's investments moved to noninterest-bearing accounts at the central bank;
- direct quantitative limits; depositing at the central bank part of the increase of loans;
- interest-rate policies; and
- refinancing of banks by the central bank.

The focus of the monetary regulation system at the first stage will be the withdrawal of a part of the banks' funds and their redeposit in the Union Reserve. This will increase or decrease the liquidity of the banks, affecting the supply of deposits by commercial banks and, consequently, control of the quantity of money and inflation.

To conduct tough monetary policies, reserve requirements on the order of 5-10 percent of the banks' deposits will be deemed initially sufficient, taking into account the decrease in budget expenditures and loan funds, and the increase in interest rates.

As reserve requirements will only be fully operational in December, the full burden of restrictive policies in October will be borne by a direct limitations on loans — a 5 to 10 percent administrative limitation on direct loans to enterprises, or by the obligatory deposit of surplus loan sums in special accounts of the central bank.

Equally important will be the interest-rate policy. In the first five to six months starting in October a new structure of interest rates will be introduced (with long-term rates higher than short-term, and loan rates higher than deposit rates) and their average level will be increased. This will limit the demand for credit and decrease noncash money growth. After five to six months interest rate policy will be liberalized (starting with loan rates).

For the public's savings accounts, interest will be raised to 4 percent annually in October and to 5 to 7 percent depending on the terms, from January 1. Later, in case inflation is high, indexation of deposits is suggested. All additional deposits starting October 1 will be deposited under commercial conditions, thus compensating for higher interest rates. For deposits smaller than 10,000 rubles, interest rates will continue to be regulated by administrative measures.

A system for refinancing will begin to operate. Funds withdrawn from banks via various methods will be loaned back to them with established interest rates depending on the monetary policy, so that the banks will be forced to link their interest rates to those of the central bank (which will be the same for all members of the Union Reserve System).

State policy can be implemented through the credit guarantees of the Union Reserve, some types of loans (exports, priority industries, small firms) can be subsidized through the establishment of specialized credit and loan institutions, and by providing the banks with incentives to competition.

The ruble must be the only legal means of payment in the Soviet territory. The issuing of any other currency and the circulation of foreign currency as legal tender must be banned in the interest of increasing the stability of the ruble.

Estimates show that the public owes up to $2 billion, equivalent to 40 billion rubles (according to the present black market rate), compared to 110 billion rubles in circulating cash. The use of foreign currency will decrease the value of the ruble faster than any growth in the supply of money or credit.

To correct this, the decree on retail trade for foreign currency issued by the Council of Ministers of the USSR will be revoked, all hard currency stores will be transformed into commercial shops (excluding extraterritorial ones in airports), the free selling and buying of foreign currency will be allowed, hard currency accounts will be opened, and other measures for internal convertibility of the ruble will be introduced.

The central element in restructuring the current system is transformation of the mechanism of issuing money. The central control of the money supply will be eliminated, as well as the inefficient cash planning.

The current system results in delays in paying wages even if an enterprise has money in its bank account. The nonfungibility between cash and money-on-account (with exchange rates as high as 1:3) leads to corruption and abuse of position, and to using bonds as money.

Issuing cash should take the form of cash sales by the Union Reserve members to commercial banks. Under such a system the central bank will issue cash by replacing money-on-account with cash; in other words the total will not be changed.

Concurrent with the tight regulation of the funds of enterprises, the separation of money into cash and noncash, which never leaves bank accounts, will be eliminated in 1991. For that aim:

- the restrictions against payment-on-account will gradually be lifted;
- limitations will be imposed on cash payments in amounts higher than 1000 rubles;
- targets for the development of noncash operations are to be determined (including higher charges for banking operations with cash, making them unprofitable);
- there will be a public campaign to encourage placing money in savings accounts.

THE STATE BUDGET

A key point in the transition to the market is a strict financial policy, meaning a sharp decrease in budgetary spending which is one of the main sources of instability.

Cutting spending. The Union and republican budgets have possibilities for cuts:

- industrial investments (20 to 30 percent) including projects started in 1990;

- expenditures of secondary importance, those that have lost their importance due to changes in policy;
- elimination of all investment projects that cost more than 100 million rubles;
- Defense Ministry (10 percent) and KGB (20 percent) budgets;
- foreign aid (70 to 80 percent);
- balances cut by 5 to 10 percent for republican budget spending on management, administration, all other budget-supported agencies (except medical);
- subsidies for unprofitable enterprises (a minimum of 30 to 50 percent);
- mass auditing of the efficiency of budget-supported agencies with elimination and cuts.

For the period up to January 1, 1991, the task will be to cut the budget deficit to less than 5 billion rubles in the fourth quarter. Complete elimination of the Union budget deficit by March 1, 1991.

An important role in balancing the budget can be played by increased income: taxation on goods turnover, introduction of other new taxes, etc.

Budget structure reform will be conducted, including the separation of budgets. All republics are to establish their own budget systems and be responsible for balancing their budgets. The balanced All-Union budget will be maintained as a rule.

Spending for social purposes and culture will become the responsibility of the republican and especially the local budgets. Local budgets will not be allowed to rely on subsidies from the republican and Union budgets.

The republics agree on the general budget policies: one of the policies is an acceptable level of deficit, with financing only via the actual placing of bonds.

There will be a fixed principle that the Council of Ministers is the only organ to plan spending, with the Supreme Soviet having the right to approve or reject proposals, with rejection amounting to a vote of no confidence. The period of time during which the Supreme Soviet analyzes the proposed budget is to be increased. There will be a rule effectively fixing the maximum amount acceptable for the deficit or the deficit is prohibited.

Items in the budget will be designated as protected or unprotected. The protected ones are linked to price indexes. All budget-financed projects costing more than 100-150 million rubles are approved by the Supreme Soviet individually.

To increase the efficiency of budget spending, republican control organizations are to be established under the auspices of the Supreme Soviet. These organs will have the right to discontinue the financing of specific projects and organizations in cases where they see negligence, abuse, or violation of terms.

The annual budget is supposed to serve as the main program-setting document of state economic policy. Key decisions on the economic events of the year are supposed to be made at the time when the budget is approved.

TAXATION

Each republic has the right to have a tax system of its own. However, inside a uniform economic area, major differences in tax systems can lead to undesirable consequences, e.g., manipulating taxation regimes, double taxation, etc. Therefore the republics will have to coordinate the basic principles of their tax systems.

At present the republics hold the view that the Union budget must be formed on the basis of funds turned over by the republics to the Union for the exercise of those powers that are delegated to it. The contribution of each republic to the Union budget is determined on the basis of its gross national product (GNP), or per capita GNP. Linking republican contributions to their per capita GNP would serve to level out the initial conditions of the transition to market relations.

Thus all economic units, both physical and legal persons, in the territory of a republic will pay taxes only to the republican and local treasuries. The distribution of tax revenue between republican and local budgets will be regulated by the legislative acts of the Union republics.

The seeming advantage of the so-called one channel method of forming budgets by regular contributions is not borne out by detailed analysis. The need to make day-to-day payments out of the Union budget, the requirements for high reliability, and the difficulties and contradictions arising when the contributions of the republics have to be decided — all of these factors make it impossible to approve this method.

A federal Union tax and its rates can be decided by agreement of all the republics. It will be possible for the Union to plan its spending on the basis of expected revenue and to bear full responsibility for its financial policy.

Under this system republics can make fixed contributions into certain projects or special funds.

A Union law on taxes is proposed as the basis for republican legislation on taxes in 1991. It envisages three basic types of taxes: a personal income tax, an enterprise income tax, and a turnover tax on goods. Still, the following amendments need to be made:

(a) the turnover tax in 1991 will be separated into a general turnover tax and special sales taxes, levied on a limited range of goods when they are sold to the public (liquor, tobacco, cars, luxury items); general turnover taxes are spread over a broad range of items, and the rates are not high, and are calculated as a proportion of sales price for large groups of products;

(b) the income tax is made uniform; special status of banks, consumer societies, enterprises of public organizations, and progressive taxation depending on profitability are eliminated; a system of tax rates tied to the amount of income is established; in calculating the income taxes of joint-stock companies, deductions are permitted for funds that are directed into reserve funds (within certain limits); the number of tax benefits is decreased, many of them to be reconsidered on an annual basis;

(c) personal income tax rates are decreased, the maximum limit of untaxed income is increased, and the rate progression depending on income level becomes less steep; and

(d) the principles of transferring funds from the republican budgets into the Union budget are altered in accordance with the terms of the Treaty on Economic Union.

A special tax is introduced for the use of nonrenewable natural resources.

Besides, as the powers of the revenue services are increased (they become truly independent), measures are to be taken to ensure that all kinds of income are eligible for taxation. Serious criminal penalties will be introduced for tax evasion.

GOVERNMENT DEBT

The internal government debt of the USSR reached 400 billion rubles on January 1, 1990. Just 20 billion are accounted for by voluntary loans. Other funds were appropriated from the banking system (350 billion rubles), most of it for undetermined periods and without the payment of interest. Twenty-two billion rubles were appropriated from the system of State Insurance (Gosstrakh) of the USSR. An attempt to issue bonds in 1990 was a complete failure, and as a result of writing off bad debts and the further appropriation of bank funds, total government debt increased by 30 percent.

It is proposed that all resources appropriated from the banking system before September 1, 1990, be transformed into long-term loans with specified conditions, as a sum transferred from the Savings Bank of the USSR to the State Bank of the USSR. The newly issued bonds will be divided among the savings banks and insurance companies of the republics as their assets, in proportion to their contributions. The writing off of agricultural debt (70 billion rubles) will take the form of reductions of the Union loan fund when it is divided between banks. The servicing and repayment of accumulated debt will become the responsibility of the republican budgets. The total sum of the Union debt will be fixed and any new debts will be allowed only upon agreement of the republics. If permission is granted, the Ministry of Finance will be the agency responsible for issuing bonds.

By consent of the republics, the program of government borrowing from the population and enterprises planned for 1990 should be carried on, with bonds being sold at market prices. To stabilize the situation and withdraw surplus cash from circulation, Union bonds should be issued even if the budget does not require it.

Each republic is to adopt legislation on republican government debt, determining the procedures and limits of its increase, the techniques of financing, and the powers and separation of responsibilities of the soviets at different levels. The following general principles are proposed: 1) the deficit of any republican budget may not exceed more than 5 percent of all expenditures, with the condition that bonds are sold; 2) a legislative prohibition on the administrative use of bank resources to finance debt, as well as forced loans. In special situations short-term (not more than 12 months) loans from the Union Reserve to the Union or republican budget can be considered.

The rules regulating the issuance and circulation of government securities and the management of government debt will be determined by the ministry of finance of each republic. The operations of repayment, interest payment, and refinancing are exercised by the republican state bank.

A decision to increase the debt of the republic can be made by its government, acting within limits established by the Supreme Soviet. Absolute and relative (to GNP) limits on debt are established.

The republican fund for debt repayment is established as a part of the budget; sources of incoming funds are specified, e.g., receipts from privatization.

The deficits of the republics, autonomous republics, regions, districts, and cities are to be financed by loans. Government bodies of different levels are not responsible for each other's obligations. Local soviets carry out their own financial policies guided by existing laws.

Before a full-fledged market of securities is developed, the conditions for local loans must be coordinated with the ministry of finance and the state bank of the republic; large loans (100 million rubles or more) must be coordinated with the Ministry of Finance of the USSR and the board of the Union Reserve to eliminate unnecessary competition (queuing of loans).

New securities should be directed at specific groups of investors, and the terms and the forms of loans should be diversified. The optimal term for loans at present is five years.

THE FINANCIAL MARKET

The financial market as a mechanism for horizontal movement of monetary resources, intra- and interindustry flow of capital funds, is a prerequisite for the efficiency of the economy and the banking system. A financial market is necessary to normalize the structure of interest rates, provide estimates of the financial position of borrowers, and mobilize the surplus funds of individuals and enterprises.

In October 1990, the formation of financial markets will begin at republican levels. This means:

(a) adoption of appropriate juridical acts;
(b) establishing a system for regulating the market.

The credit market will become the foundation of the financial market, comprising relations between banks, firms and individuals, interbank and commercial credit. The state bank of each republic, in accordance with the general policy guidelines of the Union Reserve, will oversee its credit market.

The formation of a securities market will proceed at the same time, including shares, bonds, and government securities; stock markets or branches of commodity exchanges will be established, and an interbank market will be developed. The prices of stocks and bonds on the financial market will reflect supply and demand. There will be new incentives to form brokerage companies for trading in securities, and auditing firms. Finance ministries of republics or special agencies to regulate securities and exchange will oversee the securities market. The Union Agency for Securities will coordinate the formation of the Union market, with the republican agencies delegating some of their functions to it.

An interbank credit and money market can be formed fairly quickly. The securities market will develop more slowly, its pace depending on the progress of privatization. It is important to reach consent among the republics before the reform, insuring the free movement of money flows and trade in securities and the coordination of activities of their regulatory organs.

3

Pricing Policies

Pricing policies during the transition period will be based on the following principles:

1. The government rejects the administrative increase of retail prices of consumer goods. It is only permissible for the government to set prices when goods are available to all who wish to buy them. If the government cannot provide enough goods at the prices it sets, it must leave it to the buyer and seller to establish the price. Government subsidies, maintaining the current low level of prices on food, are in fact all directed to the agriculture and the food industries, and the majority of the population have to buy food at the market or at cooperative stores, or be satisfied with the low-quality goods available in government stores.

   Currently, only 58 percent of the total amount of meat and meat products, 80 percent of milk, 25 percent of potatoes, 45 percent of vegetables, and 56 percent of eggs are sold through government stores. Of that, 40 percent of meat is low quality (or 23 percent of total consumption), and this is what finally appears on the counters. The remaining meat and other higher quality products are sold through special distribution systems and other networks that are inaccessible to the general public or are controlled by the shadow economy.

   An administrative increase of prices cannot balance the market and create the conditions for elimination of the distribution system.

2. **Consumer goods prices and services must be gradually liberated from administrative control.** At the same time, as a measure to protect the population, prices will be frozen until the end of 1991 on 100 to 150 specific products and services to preserve the minimum living standards of families. Republican and local bodies will place orders for production of those products, and if necessary, they will introduce rationing.

In the future, price controls will be gradually lifted with regard to specific conditions and the situation in the market. By the end of 1991 there ought to be free prices for 70 to 80 percent of the total sales volume in goods and services. In 1992 only prices for a very narrow range of goods that are basic necessities will be regulated (some kinds of bread, meat, milk, vegetable oil, sugar, basic medicines, school textbooks, transportation fees, and fees for certain communal services).

Gradual transition to free prices will make it possible to balance the consumer market and eliminate shortages. The more goods that are sold for free prices, and the greater the supply of goods, the sooner prices will stabilize and then begin to decrease. Price differentiation with respect to quality will emerge.

To prevent the acceleration of inflation, the removal of price control must be supplemented by severe financial and monetary policies: major cuts in the budget deficit, formation of a banking system able to control monetary circulation, strict financial qualifications for all firms, and protection of the people's savings.

Also important will be rapid rates of denationalization and demonopolization, development of competition, entrepreneurship, and a market infrastructure.

In case of a sharp increase in decontrolled prices, they can be temporarily frozen by a decision of republican or local bodies imposing price ceilings.

3. During the transition period the government cannot immediately cease its policy of maintaining low retail prices for some consumer goods as a measure to protect the population. Thus, some subsidies have to be preserved. However, **the system of subsidizing food prices must be radically changed.**

Subsidies for a limited range of foodstuffs must be directed only to the stores. The total sum of subsidies received will thus be linked directly to the amount of goods sold by the store.

The subsidizing mechanism will be established by the republics, depending on their population and the level of consumption. Local soviets will divide subsidies between stores (in proportion to the amount sold at fixed prices or to physical quantities). If a kilo of meat is subsidized to the extent of 3.5-3.7 rubles, which is the difference between the state and the market price, it will mean a savings of 8-10 million rubles in meat subsidies.

4. Relaxation of retail price control must be concurrent with liberalizing wholesale and purchase prices. The following discusses how this is to be achieved.

The 1991 prices for most intermediate goods will be established by contracts between the supplier and the buyer. Government regulation of wholesale and purchase prices will be preserved for:

- energy, fuel, basic raw materials, transport tariffs;
- products manufactured on state order;
- products manufactured by monopolies.

For energy, fuel, basic raw materials, and some mass produced items that are traded between republics, fixed government prices will be established that are determined on the basis of a multilateral agreement between republics and linked to amounts delivered.

Fuel, energy and raw material prices will be adjusted to account for increases in production costs.

The higher prices for energy and raw materials will be compensated to the consumers:

- in manufacturing industries - by economizing on resources, passing on the savings through the right to establish free prices for products, and
  — if the product prices are regulated, using the funds for stabilization to provide consumer rebates;
- in nonmanufacturing industries - through indexation of budget allocations;
- for the population - by indexation of their incomes.

For all other products manufactured on government orders, contractual prices will be established and determined by organs of the government contracting system and coordinated with the manufacturers, major consumers, and wholesale traders representing small consumers.

The organs of the government contracting system will have the power to approve prices even if consent is not reached.

However, they must consider the interests of producers and consumers, the possible dynamics of costs to both parties, and the level of market prices for similar products. In contracts for government orders, methods of price correction are provided for in case of an unexpected growth in production costs.

During the fall of 1990, negotiations must be arranged on contracts for government orders and pricing in groups of products and individual products. Existing list prices, prices for fuel, energy, and raw materials, established during multilateral negotiations involving republics, and calculations made by enterprises can all be used for guidance. Limitations on price growth can be set for certain periods (a quarter, a year), differentiated by type of product. The strictest limits must be imposed on final sales of consumer goods (not more than a 25 to 30 percent a year increase in list prices). They may be higher for industries with relatively high consumption of fuel, raw materials, and energy.

All parties in negotiations that may demand an increase of their prices should exercise social consciousness and the understanding of how destructive extreme demands can become.

The establishment of contract prices for products manufactured under government orders will be more complicated, because at the outset of negotiations the prices of many types of materials and components needed for production will be unknown.

In this connection it is advisable:

1. To provide for timely information on the final contract prices established at negotiations;
2. Hold negotiations to establish prices in a logical sequence starting with materials, semimanufactured products, components;
3. Whenever possible, to hold concurrent negotiations on products and those materials that are needed for their manufacturing;
4. Limit the number of products included in government orders and for which contract prices may be established through the government contract system;
5. In general contracts, to determine wherever possible the indexes for changing list prices of a group of products rather than prices for specific goods.

Price differentials to reflect quality are to be based on current differentials in list prices.

Within a month after negotiations, contract prices are to be published in special bulletins.

Great effort will be needed to organize negotiations and to complete them in the shortest possible time. Wherever the agencies of the state contract system cease to exist, their functions will have to be assumed by existing agencies of the state: the Committee for Supplies, the Ministry of Trade, the Agency for Supplies in Agriculture (Agrosnab) and the agencies responsible for pricing.

Disagreements left after negotiations will be settled through day-to-day correction of contract prices along the lines envisaged by the general contract and with the help of the stabilization funds.

Consumer goods to be sold at fixed prices can be included in state orders by republican and local bodies and purchased by trade organizations for contract prices. The difference arising between wholesale and retail prices will be compensated by subsidies out of local budgets.

The subsidy fund will rely on the following sources:

- budget revenues received from selling goods at free prices;
- the increase in turnover tax receipts because of the increase of wholesale prices;
- planned subsidies from republican budgets.

If, nevertheless, there are not enough funds for subsidies, local bodies must make decisions reducing the number of goods sold at fixed prices and must introduce the rationing of goods that are in short supply.

Market price formation must rely on organized commodities exchanges to a growing degree. Development of these elements of the market infrastructure has to be encouraged by providing benefits and tax reductions for contracts made there.

Government regulation of prices for goods not included in state orders must be limited to a list of goods approved by republican or local bodies and to goods produced by monopolistic enterprises.

The main method of government regulation of prices will require that manufacturers of goods sold at regulated prices must submit to competent government or local bodies documents justifying any price increases they plan. After a specified term, the bodies must make their decision based on qualified expert recommendations. The decision may be positive, negative, or a qualified positive. Substantial sanctions are to be applied in cases of noncompliance with a decision.

In the future, price regulation will be conducted mostly by the instruments of financial and monetary policies as well as by the method of "commodity intervention." The main goal is to limit aggregate demand by limiting aggregate money supply.

With a lack of concurrence in implementing the price reform by different republics, negative phenomena such as speculation may emerge; i.e., massive purchases of goods in regions with low prices, thus leaving their markets empty. Such phenomena will force regions either to introduce restrictive measures or to speed up price liberalization. Eventually prices will level out, which is a natural thing in market-type economies. To avoid such negative phenomena, however, it is advisable to coordinate any actions in this area, which can be done by the appropriate agencies of the republics and regions that will be charged with the task of preventing great discrepancies in prices.

An important condition for the success of any organized reform of pricing and timely correction of regulated prices and indexation of incomes of the population is the prompt establishment of an effective network for recording the dynamics of prices.

4

Living Standards, Social Guarantees, Wages and Salaries

Traditional programs for the transition to a market economy presuppose a certain decline in the standard of living of varying degrees of severity and length. Analysis has shown that another concept of such a program is also possible. The conditions for stabilization and improvement of the standard of living are already forming in the transitional period.

The new program means not merely transition to market mechanisms. It puts forward a more essential purpose — to create a socially oriented economy, to replace mere declarations of social priorities with the precise mechanisms, whose nature is clear to every individual citizen, for their realization.

The distinguishing characteristic of the proposed program is that, in certain circumstances, the drawbacks of our economic system can be turned to the cause of perestroika. The all-encompassing state ownership of property is one of these drawbacks.

The very high concentration of property ownership by the state gives it the opportunity to create the conditions for organized and comprehensive privatization. This will ensure that, from the very onset of the process there will be no estrangement of the worker from the means of production, that large numbers of people will be involved in the process of the economic reforms, and that the basis can be laid for new motivating mechanisms, the essence of which is to provide freedom of economic activity and private entrepreneurship, which means freedom for everybody to reach his or her own level of well-being.

To the same degree, the very fact of privatization in this country can be regarded as a specific shock-absorber for undesirable economic phenomena affecting the people's standard of living.

In Hungary and Poland the shock-absorbing mechanism of privatization was limited, since the level of state property in these countries had never reached the level it has reached in the USSR, and private enterprises had existed long before reform started. Proceeding from our conditions, we can be assured that due to privatization we can avoid a number of the negative processes that the people of the Eastern European countries faced while introducing their reforms.

The first thing to be done is to take a complete and detailed inventory of national resources and the ways of using them. There are enormous reserves which could make people's lives much easier in the near future or even now. These reserves are not considered in most projects of analogous programs. We had in mind, first of all, the defense industry and military equipment — the currently used as well as the stockpiled — which, thanks to global changes in the international situation, can be put to immediate use in the civilian economy.[1]

Enormous resources are either not used or are used ineffectively in working enterprises, are in the state's reserves, or in the hands of public organizations. These could also be put into economic circulation to be of use to the people practically at this very moment.

The rational and effective use of all resources which can be given by Western countries will help not only to intensify the industrial and scientific capacity of the USSR, but also to improve the situation in the consumer market.

The ability to meet the people's demand for consumer goods and services will actually have greater results than any increase in income.

What is the essence of the social orientation of the suggested system? First of all, it is **freedom** of economic enterprise for all: the farmer, the private owner, or the state enterprise team.

Freedom has its other side: the **responsibility** of everyone for the team he or she works in, for the society he or she lives in.

The basic social function of the totalitarian state is to redistribute national wealth among all of its people. The basic task of an owner is to create this wealth for himself and for society. This means that the labor activity of a worker guarantees an increase of his living standard, while an efficient economy creates the conditions for a higher level of wealth.

To provide equality of opportunity for every citizen is another characteristic feature of the program. It will be implemented through the state social guarantees system, which includes legislatively adopted forms and levels of social security. The legislative acts provide for long-term accomplishments in the fields of wage regulation, pensions, social security, free services distributed by the Fund for Social Consumption, and financial policy.

Thus, according to the program, a socially oriented market presupposes:

- freedom of economic enterprises as the basis of an increasing standard of living, with individual responsibility and a developed system of social guarantees;
- a social partnership between citizen and state, consumer and producer, worker and employer.

As for the transition period, the program carries a number of measures, which must be fulfilled by the Union republics in order to provide an effective and wide system of social guarantees. These social guarantees are the following:

- a minimum salary;
- pensions;
- grants;
- support during temporary disability;
- the right to work;
- the right to free education and medical service;
- privileges associated with conditions of labor;
- the right to housing; and
- the right to rest.

The program presupposes development of existing social guarantees, and strengthening their social basis, as well as including some principal new items. By the end of the transition period (in 500 days) the whole system of social guarantees will be based on a relatively new element — the legislatively adopted minimum living level of income based on the minimum consumer budget.

In addition, the following kinds of guarantees will be provided:

- measures to supply real substance for a nominal income, indexation;
- the right to unemployment benefits;

- the right to a differentiated minimum wage dependent on working qualifications and independent of the forms of property;
- the right of poor people to social support; and
- the right to property and income.

The adoption of the system of social guarantees as a basis of social policy presupposes working out a firm legislative base for every republic. The concrete levels and forms of the social guarantees will be defined by the republics, proceeding from the existing standard of living, the financial possibilities, and the time frame for realization of the program.

The development of a system of social guarantees presupposes the development of consumption funds. They become the main guarantee of social security for disabled people and the most important form of implementation of state social policy. The increasing effectiveness of using consumption funds presupposes a decentralization of administration, the increasing role of local organizations and enterprises in the formation and use of the funds.

Proceeding from the social orientation of the program, the elaboration of a minimum consumer budget must become the starting point of reform. It is the most important social guarantee, for it forms a general scale to define the minimum income rate. Proceeding from existing methods, the normal minimum of personal material security in 1988 in the USSR required 105 rubles per month. Nearly half of this sum was spent for food, 20 percent for all other sorts of consumer goods, and 14 percent for services. Nearly 3 rubles per month were given for cultural activities.

This formation of a minimum budget is oriented, first of all, toward the physical necessities of a person. It does not create conditions for development of the personality (see Supplement).

In the new situation, the calculation of the minimum consumer budget must be based not on beggarly demands and the minimum level of their satisfaction, but on the ability of a person to have an acceptable standard of living even with a minimal income.

In the new situation, the **minimum** consumer budget must guarantee not only the satisfaction of food and clothing needs (taking into account the liberalization of retail prices), but the ability to have an apartment, to benefit from medical services and education, to provide for disability. This is a new form of defining the value of labor which provides the worker not merely with a living wage, but the possibility of self-improvement and freedom of choice as a consumer.

The purpose of the minimum consumer budget, determining the basis for the minimum income rate, presupposes that its change will guarantee the corresponding changes in the area of distribution. The amount of money needed to provide the population with a minimum income must be regarded as the lower limit of resources necessary for the realization of social policy both in monetary and natural forms. This would actually mean a deviation from the carry-over principle and would signify the real socialization of the economy.

To include such a minimum consumer budget in the distribution system right now is practically impossible. There is not only a lack of means, but a lack of objective conditions: an abundant consumer market, offering both expensive and cheap goods, competitive retail prices, a developed system of commercial services, etc. These conditions must be fulfilled by the end of the transition period and will provide the groundwork for the complex reform in distributional relations.

Wage reform will become a basic point in the reform of distributional relations. Wages are the central element in the whole system of social security. There should be a focus on increasing the professional skills and social abilities of the workers.

The modern level of wages of the Soviet people cannot be regarded as a satisfactory one. Table 1 shows the **cost of certain goods in hours and minutes of working time** of a automobile industry worker in the USSR and abroad. As for the USSR, the calculation is made in two directions: the existing prices and the retail prices, suggested by the Soviet government.

Summing it up, we came to the following conclusions:

1. The cost of practically all the goods will be going up, even taking into consideration the pension and salary compensation to be introduced along with the new retail prices.
2. In comparison with the developed Western countries, the prices for produce and other products most in demand in the USSR cannot be regarded as low ones. If the price reform elaborated by the Soviet government is fulfilled, the gap in the standard of living among various social groups will increase even further.

In principle, the new system for compensating labor should be built in such a way as to eliminate from public discussion the question of worker exploitation. World experience has proven that the more developed the market the lower the level of exploitation. Labor will be fully compensated if the free worker is included in the system of professional movements which

Table 1
COST OF GOODS IN WORKING TIME
(for an automobile worker)

#	Item	Amt	Price av. in rubles	Working time hr	Working time min	Proj. Price rubles	w/o pay increases hr	w/o pay increases min	w/pay increases hr	w/pay increases min
1	Bread	1 kg	0.28	0	12.6	0.84	0	37.8	0	31.9
2	Beef	"	2.00	1	29.8	5.00	3	44.7	3	10.0
3	Pork	"	2.10	1	36.4	4.25	3	11.0	2	41.4
4	Chicken	"	3.00	2	16.9	4.00	2	59.8	2	32.0
5	Fresh Milk	1 l	0.28	0	12.5	0.50	0	22.5	0	19.0
6	Fish	1 kg	1.24	0	55.7	1.90	1	25.4	1	12.2
7	Butter	"	3.5	2	40.0	6.50	4	52.1	4	6.9
8	Vegetable Oil	1 l	1.65	1	15.3	2.50	1	52.3	1	35.0
9	Eggs	1	0.11	0	4.8	0.18	0	8.1	0	6.8
10	Potatoes	1 kg	0.15	0	6.7	0.38	0	17.1	0	14.4
11	Rice	"	0.88	0	40.5	1.40	1	2.9	0	53.2
12	Sugar	"	1.10	1	36.4	4.25	3	11.0	2	41.4
13	Tea	"	9.60	7	11.3	14.30	10	29.0	8	51.9
14	Coffee	"	20.00	15	16.1					
15	Oranges	"	2.00	1	31.5					
16	Men's wool suit		180.00	137	22					
17	Men's shirt (reg)		10.00	7	38					
18	Men's Coat		120.00	90	35					
19	Men's shoes		35.00	26	43					
20	Women's dress		60.00	45	47					
21	Gasoline	1 l	0.40	0	18.3					
22	2 rm apt	1 mo	12.00	9	10					
23	3-4 rm apt	"	15.00	11	7					
24	Refrigerator	1	350.00	267	6					
25	TV set (color)	1	700.00	534	12					
26	Automobile	1	6500.00	4961						

skillfully protect his social rights and labor guarantees. Likewise, the worker will be protected if the government realizes the rights of citizens to private property and to the income they receive from it.

The above requirements outline the direction for wage reforms which the republics should undertake before 1991. After establishing a minimum consumption budget, we must restructure the system of wage scales starting at their core. The new system should include wage scales and minimum salary levels which are determined by a worker's qualification level. The wage rate differentials for industry will be abolished. Modifying the system will stimulate workers to increase their qualifications and will reassure the

Table 1
COST OF GOODS IN WORKING TIME
(for an automobile worker) (continued)

#	USA Working Time hr	min	Germany Working Time hr	min	Italy Working Time hr	min	China Working Time hr	min	Malaysia Working Time hr	min
1	0	5.8	0	11.5	0	19.0	0	18.8	0	47.5
2	0	13.0	1	6.0	2	0	1	15	2	47.0
3	0	17.0	0	42.3	1	28.0	0	52.3	1	23.0
4	0	9.0	0	19.5	0	49.8	0	37.5	1	7.0
5	0	5.3	0	4.5	0	8.3	0	40.5	0	39.3
6	0	20.3	0	55.5	3	3.0	0	30.0	1	23.0
7	0	22.8	0	33.5	1	50.0	1	11.0	2	37.0
8	–	–	0	15.5	0	25.5	0	24.8	0	59.5
9	0	0.3	0	1.0	0	1.5	0	1.8	0	3.5
10	0	2.8	0	3.0	0	5.8	0	15.0	0	19.0
11	0	4.5	0	24.3	0	18.3	0	11.3	0	25.5
12	0	3.5	0	7.3	0	16.8	0	22.5	0	26.3
13	–	–	2	34.0	2	12.0	6	0	4	17.0
14	0	33.8	1	30.0	2	0	11	55.0	25	5.0
15	0	5.8	0	9.3	0	8.8	0	22.5	0	53.0
16	10	45	20	15	42	45	87	15	129	0
17	1	30	2	30	4	15	3	45	6	0
18	10	15	14	30	42	45	11	15	69	30
19	2	15	6	15	8	30	12	30	15	0
20	2	30	18	30	30	30	8	0	22	45
21	0	1.0	0	3.5	–	–	0	13.5	0	21.3
22	21	30	24	45	36	30	56	00	119	0
23	24	30	32	30	70	0	87	15	198	30
24	19	0	35	0	67	0	214	00	476	0
25	31	0	97	0	134	0	187	00	516	0
26	753	0	–	–	1463	0	3490	000	7143	0

worker that society protects him. In addition, the new system forces a more rational utilization of the labor force.

The system should take account of working conditions through the use of government standards and should adjust wage scales and salaries accordingly.

Minimum wage scales and salary levels are necessary for all enterprises, irrespective of the type of ownership. There is to be a minimum wage level below which a worker cannot get paid, no matter what type of enterprise.

Indexation is aimed at supplying the monetary incomes of the population with real content on the level of social guarantees established by the state.

The index of consumer prices is the most representative one in terms of a system for regulating the income of private individuals.

The selection of consumer goods and services, used for the calculation of indexes, is the principal question. It must include goods reflecting a widespread structure of consumption in a concrete period and on a concrete territory.

In modern conditions, the index "basket" can be formed on the basis of the existing minimum consumer budget and be limited by the goods in current consumption. The methods for creating this consumer price index must be the same within each republic.

The question of the correction for inflation in the cost of free services is of special interest. The periodic revision of existing monetary norms in the field of free services, in accordance with the inflation rates, can be regarded as a rather useful one.

Since the indexation is not directly connected with the quality, quantity, and the results of labor, it is important that the indexation system does not deform the wage system.

The program presupposes the strengthening of the social security of the population by the end of 1990, on the basis of economic and legal methods. First of all, it concerns the poorest social groups, large families, the disabled, pensioners, and students.

To reach this aim the program would introduce a system of private income indexation as of December 1, 1990. Payments from the funds for social consumption (pensions, grants, all sorts of support), as well as fixed incomes in the nonproductive spheres, should be given an index tied to the retail price index at the expense of the budgetary allotments. In order to balance the salaries in productive and nonproductive spheres, the salary corrections in the nonproductive sphere can be regarded as dependent not only on the consumer prices, but also on the wage index in the productive branches.

Compensation for rising living costs for workers of state enterprises will be achieved by periodically increasing the wage fund in accordance with the consumer price index. Profit-after-tax is the **basic source of income** for profitable enterprise. Unprofitable enterprises may need budget subsidies in order to compensate for the pay increase for the workers. Together with the indexation of national incomes the indexation of the private savings of the population will be introduced.

The mechanisms of nominal income indexation will be detailed during the program's realization. They will depend on the financial situation and the consumer goods market, and will be determined by the success of the stabilizing period.

EMPLOYMENT IN THE USSR ECONOMY

(a forecast on condition that the program is fulfilled completely and in due time)

	1.1.90	Changing work (DURING 1 YEAR)	Having found work	1.1.91	Changing work (DURING 6 MONTHS)	Having found work	1.7.91	Changing work (DURING 6 MONTHS)	Having found work	1.1.92
Labor resources	164			164.70			165.10			165.40
Employed in economy	139.30			139.70			138.10			134.80
Not employed including:	24.70			25.30			27.			30.60
students	11			11			11			8
Not working	7.70			8						8
unemployed including:	6	17	16.70	6.30	10	8.30	8	15	11.40	11.60
constantly unemployed	4.50			4.70			8			6.10
frictionally unemployed	1.50			1.60			3			5.50
Average period of being unemployed (months)	1			1			1.50			2
Average on functional unemployment (Rbls per month)	No			No			200			200
Total benefit on frictional unemployment (mil. Rbls)	No			No			2000			4500
Average benefit on constant unemployment Rbls per month	No			No			100			100
Total of benefits on constant unemployment (mil. Rbls)	No			No			3000			3660
Total of benefits on unemployment (mil. Rbls)							5000			13160
Expenditure for employment service and organization of public works (mil. Rbls)							2000			3500
Total of expenditures for employment service (mil. Rbls)							7000			16660

Remarks: "Frictional unemployment" means the temporary unemployment of labor resources resulting from job changes.

Free prices will be introduced systematically under special controls. Preserving low prices on essential goods coupled with income indexation will tend not to provoke negative results. In order to prevent sharp price increases, regular authority over consumer markets will be set up.

Should unfavorable trends develop or nominal incomes be deliberately restrained, then commodity interventions will be implemented. To this end, stores of cheap consumer goods, including imported ones, will be created. As a result, even a nominal reduction of incomes can be accompanied by an increase in real income due to the growth of the purchasing power of the ruble.

In the transitional period certain groups—primarily senior citizens living alone, pensioned and disabled persons, orphans, and large families—must become the targets of special social programs. By means of these programs their vital needs in food, housing, medical care, and other services should be satisfied. Special services should be created at the local level (in local soviets) for carrying out such programs, encouraging the participation of public and religious organizations in their activities.

At the first stage, while the situation in the economy is unstable, such funds should come from local budgets. Subsequently, contributions from local enterprises would apparently play a bigger role in this process.

Within the framework of those special social programs, it would be worthwhile at the initial stage of the transitional period to satisfy the most vital needs of these groups by rationed distribution of goods in natural form.

The directions and forms of putting special social programs into effect can be seen in the following table (Table 2).

How to determine the amount of resources necessary for each such social program is a separate question. The existing social statistics do not allow a detailed analysis of the living standards of different groups of the population and regional differences. Changes in this area are taking place slowly. The budget analysis of populations should be improved, with consideration of regional differences; regular selective analysis should be introduced; special price observation services should be founded, etc.

The current lack of initial data makes it impossible to form a correct estimate of the amount of resources necessary to maintain living standards in the republics. The estimates will have to be compiled while fulfilling the program together with the reconstruction of statistics agencies in the republics.

Demonopolization and denationalization are required for data collection and processing. Particular attention within the framework of preparation for the program should be paid to creating a **special system of social indicators.**

Table 2
SOCIAL SUPPORT FOR THE POPULATION

	FORM OF SUPPORT			ORIGIN OF RESOURCES	
Population groups needing support	Monetary	Natural	Regularity	1-republic budget 2-local budget 3-firms & organizations 4-charity	Decision making level: 1-republic 2-local
Elderly & disabled		Food	Once a week	2-social assurance	2
		Care	Constant	4-social support funds	2
		Lodging repairs	Once every 2 years	3, 4	2
		Drugs	Constant	1	1
		Goods at reduced prices	Seasonally	2-trade	2 dept. of local soviets
		Increased medical care	Constant	1	1
Children		Kindergarten (for families with 1 parent, students' families, families with 2 or more children	Constant	1,2,3,4	1,2
		food at school	Constant	1,2	1,2
		Increased medical care	Constant	1	1
	Children's benefit		Once a month	1	1
All groups of population with money income	Indexation of income		Not less than once a year	1	1
	Increase minimum wage to living wage		Once	1	1
Unemployed	Unemployment benefit		During 18 months after leaving work	1,2,3	1

POTENTIAL UNEMPLOYMENT IN 1991

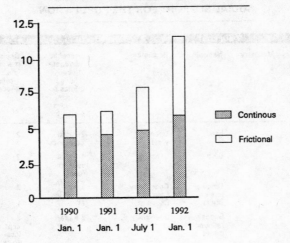

They should serve as certain barometers of social situations and trends in living standards of different social groups.

The indicators system should be composite and can include a number of traditional statistical indicators demonstrating the most painful sides of the social process, such as the movement of minimum wage rates, the number of unemployed, the price index, the inflation level and rate, the availability of consumer commodities, real incomes, real wages, etc. At the same time the investigation of public opinion on certain subjects can play an important role.

Special statistical investigations as preparatory measures are necessary before proceeding to each part of the program.

A certain set of these indicators should be carefully fixed for each stage of the program. The level of corresponding social indicators is estimated on the basis of the goals of each stage and the real situation. A deviation is a signal of undesirable tendencies and grounds for operative intervention.

Elaboration of an indicator system brings about special attention to statistics agencies as well as to services responsible for studying public opinion at every stage of the reforms.

The program of transition to a market economy, being strictly determined in time, gives to every citizen a clear-cut idea of the changes to take place at every certain period, of possibilities to open up for him as a result of those changes, and of the changes' influence on living standards and the means of

UNEMPLOYMENT

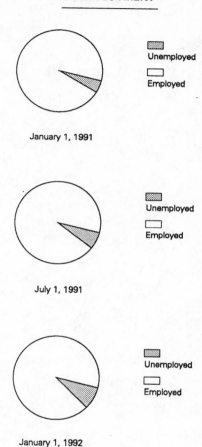

January 1, 1991

Unemployed

Employed

July 1, 1991

Unemployed

Employed

January 1, 1992

Unemployed

Employed

restricting their negative impact. The integrity of changes in all spheres of the economy provides possibilities for maintaining a standard of living and diminishing losses. But the realization of these possibilities **depends first of all on support of the program by the people and active participation of every citizen in its fulfillment, because the citizen will become the main player on the country's stage.**

5

The Labor Market

The right to work, being one of the most important human rights, must be taken as the foundation of all aspects of labor activity. Under conditions of democratic development of society, the main characteristics of employment must be appreciated in accordance with a person's interests, his or her social concern, social security, and economic condition. The goodwill of the person is a necessary condition when he or she chooses his or her way of life and determines a place for his socially useful labor, the manner of his employment and working conditions, the measure of his labor participation or the kind of professional activity.

When organizing a labor market, the greatest care must be taken for the liberation of people from compulsory labor. The right of citizens to work voluntarily, to migrate freely within as well as without this country, to freedom of choice of workplace, not depending on its territorial situation, ownership forms, or working conditions, must be legalized. All kinds of socially useful activity must be legislatively recognized as equally useful for society and be equally accessible for citizens. Any kind of activity which does not contradict the constitution and which is associated with the satisfaction of personal and social needs should be regarded as socially useful.

The program is aimed at securing an organized labor market by means of Union and republic legislation. This means the following:

First, the availability of conditions for a free choice between employment in the social production and unemployment; free choice of profession and kind of activity (with the exception of those damaging to the health and security of other citizens), taking into account both personal interests and social needs. In other words, this means freedom in supply for the labor force.

Second, freedom of all employers (in the person of state enterprises and agencies, cooperatives, leasing collectives, and so on) to hire and fire workers under the condition of obligatory fulfillment of the labor legislation rules securing the interests of citizens regarding employment guarantees, working conditions, and compensation. In other words, freedom in demand for the labor force.

Third, free movement of wages and other legalized kinds of incomes with observance of a legislatively fixed guaranteed minimum. Regulation of an upper limit on income is carried out only through a progressively scaled tax system.

A special mechanism in its turn must be created for realization of these objectives. It includes the following main elements:

- a widely accessible system of professional orientation, training, and retraining;
- a networked system of job placement centers carrying out regular registration of vacancies and job-seeking persons on the spot, settling questions of unemployment allowance payments and rendering other kinds of assistance, consultative and intermediary services to citizens in job placement, assistance to enterprises in hiring workers and settling other personnel problems and development of personnel planning;
- national and local data banks cataloging the demand for the labor force and its supply;
- special programs for stimulating the growth of employment in regions with extra labor resources, job placement assistance for different groups facing special difficulties (young people lacking fundamental professional training, women with children, invalids, released prisoners, etc.);
- a system for studying and forecasting the state of the national and regional labor markets;
- a mechanism for forming a general approach and concrete, scientifically grounded programs of regulation of professional training and employment.

According to the present program, two relative periods of labor market development may be distinguished. In the first, the transitional stage, whose main aim is to lead the economy out of the crisis and create a pluralistic market economy, the main objective of state employment policy will be strengthening the new local, economic, and social conditions of using labor resources. The second period will be characterized by stabilization of the labor market, achieving formation of a job placement network system, personnel training and retraining, and the comprehensive achievement of a social security system for the population.

It is necessary to begin immediately and set up special subprograms in all the republics.

An **employment service** under modern conditions must play a key role both in providing enterprises with the necessary specialists and in rendering assistance to workers through job placement.

At present in the USSR, along with a colossal tension in the economy owing to a shortage of the necessary labor resources, in practically all industries and professions, there are about 6.5 million unemployed persons (according to some data). Furthermore, according to the available estimates, annually about 20 percent of workers and employees change workplaces and as a consequence lose about 30 days on the average.

In the nineties the labor force of this country will be supplied by young people (more than 42 million men, or 26 percent of the total number of the population able to work). Thus, about 22 million school dropouts and about 20 million young specialists having graduated from high school and middle technical schools will have to be given jobs.

Besides, one cannot forget about demobilization from the military service and the conversion and restructuring of the economy and also about the very painful problem of refugees (forced migrants). The total burden on the job placement service may be very significant in some years. Tens of millions will need a job. Therefore a highly efficient employment service must be created and must be staffed by professionally trained and highly paid specialists.

An important place in the activity of the job placement centers must be given to systematic changes in the state of the labor market and to forecasting these changes. That will enable it to foresee forthcoming processes in the employment sphere and possible complications both in job placement and provision of the national economy and separate regions with a labor force. It will be possible to ask local executives about creating new workplaces in periods of modernization and, if necessary, postponing the date of plant closings.

A leading role in the organization of job placement services must be played by the high-profile state territorial employment centers, which can secure the collection of data both about needs for the labor force and about job seekers, and occupy themselves with their job placement and social welfare. At the same time auxiliary specialized services must be created. They will complement the activity of the territorial centers, being deeply occupied with the job placement problems of certain groups of the population. In order to properly reflect the situation in the labor market, all employment contracts should be registered at the employment services. This applies also to people who are independently employed. Companies must report to the placement service all job openings that have been filled.

It is necessary to determine, by means of laws, the legal and financial responsibility of employers for reporting inaccurate information to the job placement service centers about job openings and for concealing the facts of taking on a person without informing the job placement service.

All enterprises and organizations, independent of their form of ownership, must be placed in equal position with reference to the employment service when filling job openings and they bear equal responsibility for reporting information.

The registration of citizens needing job placement should be carried out according to the following groups of the population:

- the unemployed proper, i.e., persons who had a job but lost it because of circumstances independent of themselves;
- former pupils and students who haven't been employed by placement and haven't found a job for some other reason;
- persons who have never worked;
- persons who interrupted their work a long time ago and want to return to the labor sphere;
- persons (officers and enlisted men) who were dismissed from the military service;
- persons who have finished serving their prison sentence.

Except for the above indicated groups looking for work, it would be reasonable to permit the registration by the employment service of persons who are working but want to change jobs for some reason or other. It is possible that such services would be paid for, but they will be accessible to everybody. It is natural that priority should be given to those who are unemployed. However, for the purpose of balancing the market, providing for necessary shifts in the labor force, and for interprofessional, and interregional migration, this work must be organized immediately.

One of the most important employment services consists of securing (along with other interested parties) **guarantees and compensations for workers** being dismissed in connection with the reorganization or liquidation of an enterprise. An expansion of possibilities for preventing unemployment and a wider means of supporting people who have lost their job is an equitable requirement in such cases.

When making a decision about the large-scale layoff of workers, the administration informs the territorial job placement bureaus and the personnel themselves at a time fixed two to three months before. The persons to be dismissed are given compensation for the loss of their job in the form of severance pay for a legally fixed period (four weeks, for example), no matter whether the worker gets a new job or not.

Persons approaching retirement age are allowed to retire on a pension ahead of schedule. A variant would be the joint financing of pensions by means of the Pension Fund and Employment Fund until the workers reach retirement age.

If a new job has not been found during the period of severance payments, an able-bodied citizen has the right to an unemployment allowance.

The introduction of an unemployment allowance payment rate equal to 70 percent of the average month's wage during the first three months after the dismissal, 60 percent during the next three months, and then 50 percent for a year may be recommended as one of the possible variants.

The size of the Employment Fund and the total means necessary for maintaining living standards of the people having lost work are determined in the republics because differences in unemployment dynamics, in the structure of the unemployed able-bodied population, and differences in its degree of mobility make preliminary evaluations approximate and unreliable.

It is practically impossible to establish a uniform statute with regard to the unemployed with a list of quantitative criteria. It seems to be more reasonable that legislation of general principles and qualitative criteria be adopted for the whole country. The quantitative interpretation should belong to the competence of the republics, which, in case of need, should delegate part of their power to the regions and, possibly, to smaller territorial units. Division of responsibility strengthens the flexibility of employment policies, and raises the responsibility of territories in settling problems of job placement.

It should not be omitted, though improbable, that a worker will not find work during the time allotted and will lose the right to an unemployment allowance. It is necessary to foresee in good time the possible means of social assistance; for example, poverty allowances in money and in kind, rent and public service grants, common transport grants, and so on. A concrete list and the amount of such assistance must be established by each territory independently, with local peculiarities to be taken into account.

In the arsenal of ways of preventing unemployment it is necessary to foresee public works under contract with the municipal services of the local soviets. These works should not be limited only to construction and repair of roads and buildings - they should be expanded to all enterprises belonging to the municipality. When possible, public works may be organized at other enterprises of the territory in question. Persons employed in public works programs do not receive an unemployment allowance if the payment level at the new workplace is higher than the rate of this allowance. They are to receive the benefit of common social guarantees, including the right to pension, to temporary incapacity allowance, etc. The **state employment service** and the local executive power could share in the financing of public works. As the means assigned for these purposes by the center are limited, they should be distributed on the basis of competitions. Preference will be given to districts with a manifest abundance in the labor force.

It is inadmissible to lose sight of persons set free from the public sector of production, and possible job placement for them should be found in the cooperative and the individual sectors. A practice of granting favorable credit to everybody who desires it would stimulate such a transition.

It is obvious that a certain responsibility must be borne not only by those who have lost work but also by their former employers.

When planning a mass layoff which can sharply unbalance the labor market, it is necessary to give the employment service jointly with the local soviets the right to postpone for a term of up to six months the decision of laying-off or to veto the layoff decision. Wages for this period must be paid either fully out of the Employment Fund or through other means on a par with the enterprise's wages.

Economic units which along with a layoff organize a mass retraining of workers must receive tax benefits or a chance to cover their expenditures at the expense of the Employment Fund.

The social security system affects all working people. The economic program for the first time takes into account the specific character of various sociodemographic groups in the labor force, whose ability to compete for objective reasons is restricted.

The groups least able to compete include: people with inadequate (in comparison to others) characteristics (physiological invalids); certain age groups (young people aged from 14 to 16 years, persons approaching pension age); those with social and condition-of-life situations (women with young children, persons giving care to ill relatives); those lacking work qualification, such as persons desiring to begin to work for the first time (unskilled workers); and persons who are not employed because of the restructuring of production (the unemployed).

The system of social support must consist of two parts: social payments (pensions, unemployment allowances, other forms of social assistance) and social benefits facilitating those looking for work and hence for a stable income (reserving workplaces, learning a professional skill, specific conditions of labor payment and work rules). The relations between them depend on the concrete economic situation. But the availability of these two elements of the system is necessary because the problem of social support of the population cannot be solved with the aid of only pecuniary payments.

In this connection it is advisable:

- to enlarge the list of jobs where using the labor of women is forbidden;
- to establish quotas for enterprises and organizations to admit graduates, proceeding from the need for the employment of young people and from the perspectives for development of the specific enterprises;
- to finance expansion of the existing network of specialized enterprises, raising requirements for the labor conditions of invalids and setting benefits payments.

Among the sources for financing this social support, the dominant part should belong to the republics because now they also are responsible for the socioeconomic stability of the society. An active policy of creating the means of social assistance and also pension funds at the expense of the savings of workers seems to be premature because workers' incomes are not sufficiently high. Such an approach can have negative consequences because the relation between consumption and savings of workers is violated.

In the process of developing a market economy and, accordingly, developing a free labor market, changes in the existing practices of trade union movements will inevitably take place. The process of organizing parallel trade unions seems to be continuing. Their main task is to defend those workers with a diminishing value in the labor force from excessive intensification of labor. These new organizations of workers are assumed to be created mainly on the lower, rank-and-file level and their structures will be very diversified depending on organizational forms, particularly in the early stage. The appearance of such kinds of organizations which in their essence will not be professional ones is also possible.

At such enterprises the trade unions will fulfill their original function of defending workers' interests also mainly in the traditional manner, namely by dialogue with the management, making collective contracts, etc.

Besides, the introduction of stock ownership will open before them one more form of activity — a participation system. There will be various methods for trade unions to participate in the control of production and the economy.

Joining in such activity will permit the unions to raise their problems to a higher level not limited by their "knife and a fork" demands. They can, first of all, join in the solution of the most serious problem — overcoming the deep alienation of the worker from the means of production.

The following spheres of activity of trade unions' associations are important: dialogue with state officials on different levels; participation in state regulation of social relations on the whole as well as labor relations, in particular, by including union representatives on a par with various agencies, both consultative and plenipotentiary, which formulate and enforce the social policy of the country and the separate regions. The trade unions must play a significant role in elaborating social and labor legislation and later in carrying out their own independent control of its observance on all levels.

6

Enterprise Under Market Conditions

Transition to a market economy entails some changes in strategy and tactics for the management of each enterprise, particularly for the first enterprises to be freed or to free themselves of state control.

As soon as the main measures in the sphere of finance, credit, and money policy have been carried out, a period of decisive changes in production will begin. The primary tasks of an enterprise's management personnel will be: arranging economic contracts, and determining the product lines in which it is best able to compete. The main directions of an enterprise's activity can be most readily decided at the local level.

The new competitive conditions that are arising will be connected not only with the rise in the influence of economic risk factors but also with the advantages of free price formation, with the possibility for independent choice of suppliers and customers, with better quality raw materials, semi-finished products, finishing elements, and accessories.

The main task of enterprise management will be organizing and objectively informing each member of the company and explaining the new goals of their work. When a situation ensures collective decisions, all of the workers of the enterprise will be able to make their contribution to the most complicated decisions in full measure of their capacity.

Transition to a market economy will entail a major change of orientation for enterprise activity. The enterprise should have only economic objectives — raising the efficiency of production, maximizing profit, and conquering new markets.

No ideological factors should influence the decision-making process. The interests of the state and the republics should be a matter for the government, which can exert a corresponding regulating influence by means of economic methods.

The process of denationalizing the economy will take several years, but changes in the internal life of enterprises must occur within the next few months. There must be a principle of noninterference by powerful state bodies and political organizations in the internal affairs of enterprises, including the wage level, the staffing number, and the organization of production. This means that the concept of "sponsoring organization" disappears, i.e., the industrial ministries, chief administrators, and other superstructural bodies must lose all rights to interfere in the internal affairs of enterprises.

At the same time the government is relieved of responsibility for the state of affairs of enterprises, for the wage level of their workers (above the official minimum), for providing raw and other production materials, and for selling their product.

The functions and rights of the owners (government bodies) must be strictly limited. For state enterprises it should be the assignment of managers, for stock companies where the government holds the controlling share, the adoption of strategical decisions - assignment of managers, profit distribution, raising capital.

The manager of an enterprise must be the key figure in its control. He will be empowered in almost all questions regarding enterprise activity to bear full responsibility for the financial results of the business and for any changes in the capital entrusted to him only by the owner. Under the new conditions it is out of the question for enterprise managers to be assigned by the sponsoring organization and, all the more, by political bodies. The nomenclature system must be absolutely eliminated. At the same time elections may be held for a manager only in cases where all the workers are shareholders of the enterprise. The assignment of managers is a prerogative of the owners, who risk their money. When doing this a competition for choosing the most highly trained managers may be declared. The managers themselves will work according to fixed-term contracts, where all employment conditions are clearly defined.

Management's responsibility for an enterprise's state of affairs and the power over enterprise subdivisions is raised significantly. The abandonment of central planning greatly increases the role of corporate planning, the development of strategy and tactics for the enterprise in the marketplace. This requires strengthening all economic services, the sales and marketing subdivision, and raising the level of corporate operations. At the same time,

STRUCTURE OF SOVIET EXPORTS

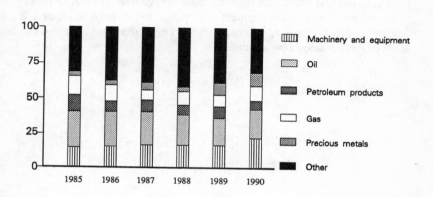

it requires new management abilities, and a quick reorganization of the business education system in each republic for meeting these practical needs.

The relationships among workers, owners, and managers within enterprises must be changed. They will be based on the assertion of interests. A new collective contract must become the main instrument of their agreement. When concluding it every year, accord must be reached on mutually acceptable solutions regarding wage increases, working rules, discipline, and the improvement of working conditions. Such an approach requires "gentlemanly behavior" by all of the parties — if an agreement is achieved, then no one may demand changing it ahead of schedule. This relates first of all to strikes.

The role of trade unions must be changed. Their function as defenders of the workers' interests and as distributors of social services must be separated. Membership in unions must be voluntary. Social guarantees to workers should not be dependent on it. Agreement on mutual interests requires the quickest application of the new ways to interest the workers in the enterprise's profit: wages will be oriented to the average market level and their growth will take into account the rate of inflation; additional pension schemes for the particular enterprise will be introduced; and favorable methods will be introduced for the acquisition of the enterprise's shares by its workers.

This economic arrangement is based on active, goal-oriented processes aiming to improve labor standards; its rational organization must be developed and a system of labor payment and quality control must be created. It is also important in any agreement with working collectives to strengthen labor discipline along new principles.

7

Opening The Economy And
Foreign Economic Policy

BASIC ASSUMPTIONS

Opening the national economy of the USSR, and its introduction into the world economic market, is one of the main goals of the reform. External economic connections are, on the one hand, important factors accelerating the transition to a market economy, and on the other hand — they are shock absorbers mitigating the negative consequences of the transition.

In order to successfully solve the problem of opening the economy and exploiting the full potential of external economic relationships, it is necessary:

- to preserve the USSR as a united economic region with a common money, finance, and currency system and common principles of regulating the activity of economic participants;

- to preserve a **unified territory of the USSR for the purposes of customs, and currency control** and uniform regulation of foreign economic relations. Otherwise, these would be the source of disintegration and disruption of the All-Union market, and they would strengthen the tendency of raising barriers that would hinder inter-republican deliveries;

- to reorient foreign relations **in the interests of developing a united All-Union market.** That means both using foreign competition and protecting individual industries, and agriculture;

- to introduce **firm state regulation** which will be principally different from the monopoly of foreign trade, via division of the functions of management and commercial activity. There will be equality of all

those involved in external economic relations with respect to the rules
and regulations of the governing bodies, which determine the generally
adopted regulatory instruments (rate of exchange, customs duties,
subsidies, taxes, interest rates, quoting and licensing standards).

Creation of legislation corresponding as closely as possible to world
practice is an important condition for the successful development of external
economic relations. This legislation must clearly define the regulating functions of the executive and legislative power on the level of the USSR, the
republics, and local state bodies. In October and November of this year the
laws and other acts concerning foreign investments, currency control and
currency regulation, foreign trade licensing, the customs system, stock
companies, and the main laws on regulation will be adopted on the All-Union
level and ratified by the republics. The latter will coordinate the corresponding republican acts with them.

All republics must agree on a uniform customs, currency, and foreign
trade policy accompanied by establishment of the corresponding All-Union
regulatory bodies.

The All-Union regulating functions, including the making of currency
policy, are carried out through the Council of the Reserve System of the
Soviet Union, the Ministry of Finance of the USSR, some new body created
on the basis of the State Currency Committee and the Ministry for External
Economic Relations of the USSR (MEER), and the Customs Control Administration. The Union republics delegate concrete functions to these
bodies. These bodies formulate general policy and are free of any commercial
activity. The bulk of practical functions within the framework of uniform
rules and policy is carried out by the republican bodies (except customs).

In 1991 external trade activity will pass in practice to the enterprise level.
Government bodies at all levels will cease commercial operations. Before
the beginning of 1991, the foreign trade associations of MEER are to be
transformed into intermediary stock companies working on a commission.
Shareholding participation is permitted for government bodies of the republics, for banks and for enterprises. The objective of such firms is to ensure
Soviet enterprises (both those who produce for export and those who are
importers) better conditions than those offered by foreign firms, to protect
the interests of our enterprises on the external market, to permit them to
realize their right of choice and to carry out exportation and importation by
themselves or through an intermediary.

During 1990 and 1991 the right to carry out international currency
operations is to be given over to the approximately 10 to 15 commercial

banks which are best prepared. Beginning in the autumn of 1990 there will be a systematic licensing of the external borrowings of enterprises and organizations of the republics by the ministries of finance. It will be done within republican quotas coordinated at the level of government.

The main sources for raising currency receipts in the transition period are connected with raising the standards of manufacturing raw materials, improving their quality, and taking favorable advantage of circumstances. For a number of exports (timber, oil and petroleum products, gold, diamonds) there are proposals to increase currency receipts without additional drawdown beyond the initial raw materials. Making inventory of these proposals and their realization is urgent, both on the level of the republics and the USSR as a whole.

There are great possibilities in the development of **labor intensive products** oriented both **for export and internal needs** through relatively simple modernization (using foreign capital) of such industries as textiles, leather, and footwear as well as assembling.

The state monopoly on exportation of such vital products as oil, gas, gold, and diamonds should be maintained for some period. This exportation will be the main source of currency resources for republican and local government bodies.

Proceeding from the real state of the Soviet economy, which is unbalanced, it may be expected that using taxes to stimulate import substitution will speed the development of the domestic market by raising competitiveness as well as the standard of living of the population. Increasing exports to generate payment for the growing imports of goods is now becoming more and more difficult. There are goods which we can and must produce by ourselves (grain, meat, rolled ferrous metal).

Import decentralization can be carried out with force. Starting in 1991 **centralized import deliveries should be sharply reduced** (including grain and equipment). For decentralized import an obligatory obtaining of licenses by the currency owners may be required. Enterprises that use state credits for imports must pay not only the principal debt, but also interest.

Under present conditions it is advisable to increase imports of consumer goods, the means of production for small enterprises producing consumer goods, food, construction materials, and equipment for retooling the engineering industry. All this is attainable on the condition that the importation of raw materials, semifinished products, and technological equipment be reduced. This process is regulated by means of foreign trade and customs policy already at the first stage of the reform.

THE EXCHANGE RATE, THE CURRENCY MARKET, AND CONVERTIBILITY OF THE RUBLE

The development of reforms must solve the problem of ruble exchange rates. By November 1, 1990, the system of differentiated currency coefficients will end and a common rate for the ruble for both trade and nontrade operations, applicable in transactions of the state with citizens and enterprises, goes into effect. Later on, this rate will be adjusted by the Reserve System of the Union, according to the state of the balance of payments, to liberalize price formation and level market rates.

The official currency market for the purpose of buying and selling currency at official rates will be complemented by a gradual development, starting in October 1990, of a **free currency market** with determination of rates on the basis of supply and demand. As the source of supply for this market, a constantly increasing part of the currency resources of the state, the currency funds of enterprises and private income will be used.

The market will be formed as an organization on the basis of representatives of banks and stock exchanges as well as numerous exchange bureaus according to general rules set by the currency control bodies. State currency resources will be sold by auction. Restrictions on transferring currency between the republics are not permitted and strict currency control will be maintained with respect to foreign countries.

A certain stabilization of the exchange rate for the ruble may be expected by the beginning of 1991 provided that the measures of the first stage are successful. By this time the restrictive monetary policy will cause the earning and selling of foreign currency to obtain rubles. Only then will the mechanism of market regulation by the Union Reserve System begin to work. By the end of 1991 the market exchange rate must be the only rate.

There are two scenarios of movement toward the convertibility of the ruble.

According to the **first** one it is necessary to create a system of **foreign currency interrelations** in the following manner:

(a)   all foreign currency receipts are transferred to the accounts of the enterprise. The state monopoly retains a fixed part of the receipts from exports of oil, gas, gold, diamonds, and a few other goods;

(b)   a part of this foreign currency must be sold at a common (obligatory) rate to republican bodies. The rate of deductions is determined by aggregate commodity items;

(c) the republican bodies transfer a part of their foreign currency to the center for the purpose of servicing the foreign debt and for All-Union needs; the rest is sold in the market or used for supporting republican programs;

(d) the foreign currency of enterprises is used for importing (provided that an import license is available), is sold in the market, or accumulates and earns interest.

The **second** way is more radical and assumes immediate withdrawal of foreign currency from the domestic economy. As its main source, **the foreign currency retentions from exports must be ended**. Enterprises would sell part of their currency receipts at a common rate to banks that are given power by republics (for further redistribution among Soviet, republican, and local government bodies). The rest of the receipts within a fixed term are sold through the free currency market. If an exporter or any enterprise wants to import something, it must receive an import license to buy currency. According to international practice the second scenario is preferable, but adopting it requires significant political will.

Citizens may freely buy and sell foreign currency and open foreign currency accounts. Transferring funds in foreign currency and dollars abroad is restricted by the rules of foreign currency control.

In fact this means introduction of limited internal convertibility of the ruble, without any provision for foreign currency payment between Soviet legal and physical persons, without foreign currency shops, i.e., without any of the elements of "dollarization," which undermines the buying capacity of the ruble. Development of a normal market mechanism is counterpoised to the erroneous principle of foreign currency self-financing. Everybody will get access to foreign currency (not only the exporters).

It seems advisable to adopt the first variant from the start of January 1991, and by 1992 (with the ripening of preconditions) to attempt to carry out the transition to the second variant.

Independent of the variant adopted, the center will lose part of its foreign currency monopoly. All-Union foreign currency reserves are to be maintained for ensuring external debt but they are **collective property**. At the same time sovereign republics may form their own gold and foreign currency reserves.

The level of rates for the obligatory selling of foreign currency to government bodies is to be agreed upon by the republics in order to create a common foreign currency policy. As market relations develop, the state's share in the distribution of foreign currency will decline.

THE INVOLVEMENT OF FOREIGN CAPITAL
AND FOREIGN DEBT

Inclusion in the world economy can be facilitated by attracting foreign capital and technology on a large scale. Such investments will produce an effect already offered in long-term perspective and reduce the period of transition.

It is in our interest to **draw in foreign investments in various forms** including having enterprises belonging completely to foreigners be registered as Soviet legal entities (stock companies) or branches of foreign companies. The acquisition (buy-out) of currently existing joint enterprises or constructions on the basis of contracts or concessions is also feasible.

Before November 1, 1990, legislation on foreign investments will be adopted for these purposes, and restrictions will be lifted on the size of foreign participation in enterprises. Companies with foreign participation will be established by simple registration and restrictions on many kinds of entrepreneurial activities will be lifted.

The "enclave" approach to the development activity of foreign capital in the USSR (creating closed "free economic zones," banking restrictions on economic operations in rubles for joint and foreign companies, attempts to elaborate special legislation for foreign investors or to guarantee the exchange of the ruble earnings of foreign partners into foreign currency for transfer abroad) does not seem to be justified.

Among measures to draw in foreign capital, the following are necessary:

1) Before the end of 1990, creating at the republican and regional level, state organizations which would work to attract foreign investors (like the former Glavkonceskom).

2) Creating new channels for attracting foreign investments in the form of **investment funds** with the participation of foreign capital. Shares of Soviet enterprises will be sold through such funds (with certain restrictions for some industries and spheres of activity).

3) Creating legislation on the **principle of equality of Soviet enterprises and foreign investors**. The economic activity of foreign investors on the territory of the USSR should be determined mainly by the general legal regulations of Soviet economic law. Accordingly, **free economic zones** should be developed in those regions

where the dismantling of the administrative system is proceeding most at the fastest pace.

4) Immediate permission for **ruble operations within the USSR** (without the right to export) for foreign firms. This measure would lead to an increase in the demand for rubles (which is a condition of future convertibility) and encourage foreign enterprises to reinvest their profits in rubles gained in the USSR and not strive to export them abroad in foreign currency.

Granting tax and other benefits to foreign investors requires a **flexible approach reflecting the specific character of industries**. The effect from foreign investments is expected to be maximum in such sectors as:

- the agricultural-industrial complex, including the food industry and machinery for agriculture;
- wood processing and the pulp and paper industry;
- the information technologies, the production of computers and modern communications equipment;
- the commercial sphere (the domestic wholesale and retail trade, and the banks).

Stimulating foreign business should not be restricted to tax allowances. **A complex system of attracting foreign capital** must be created on the basis of clear political guarantees, with training for specialists, and preparation of the infrastructure, delivery and communication systems. This task should be solved by special republican bodies occupied with attracting foreign investments.

The possibility of granting large economic and financial aid to the USSR in volumes of 10-20 billion dollars is being discussed in the West. One of the key questions is connected with the mechanism for distribution of the foreign currency and material resources given to the USSR. The question does not concern the political conditions of the aid, but involves those guarantees which would ensure its efficient use, and that of qualified, independent consultants' investigations of projects. The structures being created in the process of aid realization (in particular, investment and other fund distribution organizations) could help shape market practices.

These following channels are admissible.

The first channel: Foreign aid (first of all, food aid) is received and the goods are sold at state prices and the receipts are transferred into special accounts. The use of such means for crediting the private sector is carried out according to agreements with the West. Sales of consumer goods goes through the existing trade network and through specially created trade firms. Such large-scale aid is possible only in the case of adoption of a radical program of reforms and a joint appeal of M. Gorbachev and B. Yeltsin to the West.

The second channel: Foreign currency loans are received immediately by enterprises underwritten by international funds created within the framework of the aid program both abroad and in the USSR. Such funds should have independence in setting conditions on the terms of lending and repayment. The activity of the funds is carried out in communication with government bodies of the USSR. However, there will be no guarantees from our side.

The third channel: International monetary and finance organizations like the IMF, IBRD, and others would play a key role. This source could dispense significant long-term resources but it also depends on achieving a consensus within the USSR.

In October 1990, it is intended to start negotiations on behalf of the USSR and all the republics with the leading countries of the West and international organizations for the purpose of requesting aid and long-term loans for the reform program. The negotiations may lead to a new Marshall Plan.

The external debt of the USSR is a great problem. Its net value in 1989-90 has more than doubled. Each citizen of the USSR owes over 100 US dollars to Western banks.

The balance of payments of the USSR has permanently deteriorated, both because of negative influences on world prices and internal factors (shortfalls in the volume of oil extracted). The total yearly deficit in foreign trade will reach 10 billion rubles. At the same time the possibilities for foreign borrowing have been almost exhausted. A reduction of short-term credits has not been balanced by other loans. Under these conditions there must be an additional increase in the sales of gold, diamonds, and other goods, along with a decreasing level of foreign currency reserves. All this leads to a sharp rise in the cost of borrowing.

In 1991 the foreign trade deficit must be decreased to 3-6 billion rubles as a result of changing relations with East European countries (there will be a transition to convertible currency).

It is obvious that the balance-of-payments problem will not be solved without:

- stopping the direct (planned) distribution of foreign currency by the government (the foreign currency plan is transformed into the forecast of the balance of payments);
- eliminating remnants of the foreign currency monopoly, i.e., recognizing the property rights of exporters to foreign currency;
- making a clear division of functions and power between the center, the republics, the enterprises, and citizens.

The balance-of-payments deficit should be eliminated in 1991 as a result of the new exchange rate policy, the regulation of goods and capital loans, the creation of incentives for foreign capital, and new approaches to foreign debt.

The level of accumulated debt of the USSR attained by October 1, 1990, should be fixed and thereafter only refinancing will be allowed. Then it will be necessary to organize negotiations to elaborate a formula for the participation of each republic in paying off the debt. It is advisable to determine the concrete share of each republic without a juridical division of the total sum of debt. All new All-Union borrowing must be carried out by agreement of the republics.

The government's official foreign borrowings must be strictly separated from commercial foreign borrowings. Official borrowings are accomplished on behalf of governments for completing reserves, commercial borrowings — directly or on commission from concrete organizations, enterprises, and local government bodies.

External borrowing regulations depending on the state of the balance of payments of the country are to be introduced. Every year limits on the growth of both official and total external debt are to be set, proceeding from the indicators of debt level adopted in international practice. In connection with the present situation, the limits of the total sum of external debt must be set immediately and the quotas for the republics must be determined.

A system is to be developed for **commercial borrowings**. Under this system, in accordance with the annual limits, the receipt of foreign loans is to be licensed by the currency control bodies within the framework of the rules and quotas. Competition for licenses is to be organized and priorities established. The governments do not bear responsibility for such borrowings.

Attempts to independently attract significant loans by the republics are still risky. It is advisable to make use of the prestige of the USSR in international markets. The following problems are especially important:

- improving the maturity structure of the foreign debt (reducing its short-term portion);
- commodity credits (interventions) in the size of 2-3 billion dollars at the end of the first 100 days of the reform;
- stimulating new enterprise structures.

To reduce the financial claims of the USSR on other countries, some measures are to be taken. In 1990-1991 foreign currency or consumer and other goods in excess of a planned 5-10 billion rubles (at domestic prices) should be received as repayment of credits, even with enormous rebates from the nominal debt sum. At the same time the aid of the USSR to other countries is to be reduced by 70 to 80 percent (except humanitarian aid).

FOREIGN ECONOMIC ACTIVITY

Our foreign economic activity should be fully deideologized. **A uniform foreign currency and trade policy** will be observed in relations with all countries. With each partner we should take into account **purely economic and commercial factors**. This means a transition in 1991 to payments in freely convertible currency and at world prices with all countries including Finland, Yugoslavia, and Cuba. From intergovernment cooperation we shall pass to purely commercial cooperation.

Relations with the COMECON countries are now based on the absence of any future for this organization. It is evident that in a short-term plan these countries want to make use of the USSR only to mitigate the process of reorienting their economies toward the West. It is not admissible to maintain any form of clearing and price inequality with the COMECON countries. Commodity trade with this group of countries will inevitably be reduced to an optimal level.

It is advisable to arrange advantageous trade relations with all countries without exceptions (in particular the Republic of South Africa should be included). We must take into account the long-term historically shaped traditions in our relations with various countries. We must make active use of contacts with Russians and representatives of other nationalities living abroad to promote business cooperation. With the beginning of the realization of the program of transition to the market economy, discussion will begin on the subject of joining the IMF, IBRD, BIS, Asian Development Bank, GATT, and other organizations, and negotiations will be started. The process will take a long time. However, it will reveal the position of the leading Western countries regarding the conditions of entry (including the necessity of Soviet domestic reform). In any case, this will accelerate the receipt of necessary consultations and other forms of aid and, ultimately, the transition to a market economy.

8

The Shadow Economy

Now, in connection with the deteriorating economic situation in the country, the scale of the shadow economy has grown and this is causing popular protests and numerous demands to put an end to its influence upon government bodies and other social institutions. Many people associate the flourishing of illegal shadow economic activity with the transition to a market economy.

However, the true situation is quite different. The shadow economy is a necessary supplement for the administrative command system. The more the mechanisms for distribution of goods substitute for normal trade, the larger the sphere of activity is for the shadow economy. Transition to a market economy is the most efficient way to liquidate the shadow economy. The vagueness and the differences in interpretation of the concept "shadow economy" require a brief formulation of this concept and an estimate of its scale.

A shadow economy is defined as production, distribution, exchange, and consumption of goods and services that are not controlled by society. In other words, it includes socioeconomic relations between various citizens and social groups making use of state ownership for mercenary motives and hidden from government authorities. It comprises all unregistered, non-regulated kinds of economic activity different from those which are shown in juridic documents and rules.

The actual practice of planning the national economy has become hopelessly removed from real life and economic conditions. Strict enforcement of all the laws and other acts now in effect would lead to a full production stop. One may state that the shadow character of the Soviet economy is rapidly growing.

THE STRUCTURE OF THE SHADOW ECONOMY

The criminal economy is built into the official economy (bribery, theft, and other mercenary crimes); clandestine economic activity is concealed fully from all forms of control (drugs, gambling, prostitution); crimes against the personal property of citizens are an illegal form of income redistribution (robbery, gangsterism, theft of personal property, rackets).

The fictitious economy is the official economy providing fictitious results reported in the actual accounting system as real ones.

The informal economy is the system of informal interactions between economic individuals based on personal relations and direct contacts between them and supplementing or replacing the organized system and process of economic relations which is officially in force.

The nonlegalized second economy comprises concealed and uncontrolled business by individuals and cooperatives, i.e., those which are either prohibited by law or not registered or not reported in full volume in the accounts.

The above elements are not strictly isolated from each other and the borders between them are vague. The redistribution of resources from one sector to another is an ordinary business. Noncriminal methods pass ambiguously into the criminal.

In the context of the present program, the size of the shadow economy is of special importance, because, by the logic of transition to a market economy, the utilization of shadow capital is in the interest of the whole country. It is an important factor for supplying resources for the reform.

It is important to stress the necessity of evaluating the various phenomena of the shadow economy because their economic substance is heterogeneous and does not permit a mechanical addition of partial estimates in order to obtain a general idea about the size of shadow economy. It is necessary to delimit the volume of goods circulating in the shadow economy and the incomes of participants in the shadow economy.

According to the above, we shall give some estimates of a number of phenomena of the shadow economy which are available — the fictitious economy. As the Gosplan of the USSR shows in repeated calculations, the fictitious economy provides 36 to 40 percent of the value of consumer products, i.e., about 600 billion rubles in 1989.

Nonproductive costs and losses in 1988 were about 40 billion rubles (according to the Goskomstat of the USSR).

By the estimates of the Research Institute of the Ministry for Internal Affairs of the USSR (RIMIA), the output of products of inferior quality now reaches 110 billion rubles and falsified reports of output reaches 15-30 billion rubles. The losses from possible theft of public property is estimated to be 5.2 billion rubles. Every year legal institutions reveal 240,000-280,000 mercenary crimes in the economy. The losses from them are 200-250 million rubles. Some 250,000-300,000 persons take part in these crimes. Seven to 12 percent of the total number of crimes are committed by groups. There is clearly a fixed tendency for the association of economic crime with other types of criminality — its character is interindustry and interregional.

Every year 1.4-1.6 million people are held responsible for corrupt administration and breaking the law, including small plunder (780,000-800,000), illegal use of cars and machinery (550,000), illegal self-employment (45,000-46,500).

Here are estimates of other phenomena of the shadow economy:

- artificial shortage — 40 billion rubles (All-Union Conjuncture Institute), concealing goods from the open trade — 6 billion rubles (Research Institute of the Ministry for Internal Affairs (RIMIA)),
- defrauding buyers — 10.7 billion rubles (Goskomstat USSR), 4.4-9.8 billion rubles (RIMIA);
- the illegal service industry on the whole — about 14-16 billion rubles (Economic Research Institute of the Gosplan of the USSR);
- charging illegally high prices — 1.2-1.5 billion rubles (Goskomtsen of the USSR);
- speculation in cars — 5.7 billion rubles, in spare parts for auto service — 1.0 billion rubles;
- income from speculation in nonfood accommodation — 1.3 billion rubles, in alcoholic drinks — 0.1 billion rubles (Goskomstat of the USSR);
- theft of public property — 3.1 billion rubles, petty theft — 1.8 billion rubles (Goskomstat of the USSR) home-brew production — 23.0 billion rubles, including sales — 9.0 billion rubles (Goskomstat of the USSR);
- bribing government officials by cooperators — 10 billion rubles, by the citizens when receiving, exchanging, and alienating wells, garages and garden lots and also when organizing public services and amenities — 1.0 billion rubles (Goskomstat of the USSR);
- prostitution — 0.7 billion rubles; trafficking in narcotics — 0.3 billion rubles (Goskomstat of the USSR);
- unearned wages and salaries and undeserved bonuses for fictitious work (losses, falsified output reports, output of unacceptable quality production) — about 30-35 billion rubles (RIMIA).

Thus, according to all the sources from which estimates are available, income from the shadow economy equals 66-146 billion rubles. A higher estimate of this income is 175 billion rubles, calculated by comparing the international standard for the personal consumption ratio of the gross national product with the wage and salary fund ratio of the national income at the domestic level of this indicator. This permits an estimate of the shadow economy income equal to 20 percent of GNP. Also, material resources amounting to several tens of billions of rubles are circulating in the shadow economy.

The main cause of the existence of the shadow economy on this scale in our country is the absence of private property as a means of production and the predominance up to now of command and administrative methods when managing the activity of economic participants. One of the factors creating a prominent role for the shadow economy is the equilibrium between the demand prices, which the consumer is ready to pay, and the administrative shortages and administrative distribution of commodity goods. Under conditions of shortages, stable prices have many advantages for those who have privileged access to goods, while the rest of the population is forced to pay increased prices or to spend time looking for goods and standing in lines. Furthermore, the creation of artificial shortages is becoming profitable.

In essence, the rise and development of the shadow economy to a considerable degree appears as a fitting reaction to the excessive regulation of economic activity, limiting the initiative of individual workers and the independence of economic organizations.

Accordingly, the main measures for eliminating the shadow economy coincide with the most important direction of reform.

As world experience shows (including that of the countries of Eastern Europe) over 90 percent of the operations of the shadow economy can be removed rather quickly with the aid of measures for market reform. Practically at once the tremendous mass of nonsanctioned operations of the state economic units can be eliminated if centralized planning and the state ownership monopoly are given up.

The program proposes the adoption on the republican and All-Union levels of decisions which will undoubtedly ensure:

- the formation of a "middle class" while privatization is proceeding under conditions of maximum publicity and under the soviets at all levels;
- the creation of a strong tax inspection service by attracting the corresponding forces of the KGB and the MVD. Beyond significantly

strengthening the tax inspection service, this measure will begin the "conversion" of the KGB and the MVD and it will undoubtedly have positive social results;

- lawful and practical defense of citizens' and working collectives' property rights, both the means of production and the income from it. For this purpose special law-enforcement teams of the national guard type should be formed, with clearly defined functions;

- overcoming monopolism in the economy, in particular, by introducing higher tax rates, price restrictions for the production of the monopolists, and other methods defined by antimonopolistic legislation;

- the gradual introduction into practice of yearly income declarations to the tax inspection service. Adjusting the size of the total annual tax payment (made monthly at highly progressive tax rates) according to the data of the annual declaration should neutralize the tendency of citizens to avoid declaring any extraordinarily large legal income because of the high monthly rates;

- as much as possible, reduction of the special systems of distributing consumer products (vouchers, warrents, inside sales, etc.) and ensuring full openness and prudence in such cases where those systems are of vital importance (for babies and various categories of disabled men and women). This will by itself reduce the size of the shadow (uncontrolled) distribution and also remove any possibilities for free-loading on officially adopted closed distribution systems by those persons who are occupied in such distribution;

- eliminating such organizational monopolies as the industrial ministries and, first of all, depriving them of the distribution and redistribution of power; dismissal of most middle-ranking management bodies;

- reforming the laws and adopting criminal, civil, and administrative legislation which provide scientifically grounded criteria for criminalization and decriminalization of activities in the economic sphere, with higher penalties for the most dangerous kinds of economic crimes (organized criminal activity, concealing incomes from taxation, laundering income received through crime), and elaborating a law on preventive measures against breaking the law in the economy.

When the program is elaborated in detail, calculations can be made regarding the concrete amounts to be received from converting shadow capital and incomes to the national economy and the people's consumption.

NOTES FOR PART II

1. A concrete analysis of these reserves was greatly hindered by the lack of complete data for our working group.

PART III

STRUCTURAL POLICY AND CONVERSION

1

Structural Reorganization in the Sphere of Investment

An appraisal of the current structure of the economy can be summed up as follows:

The economic structure is utterly unbalanced: the investment, defense and mining industries are excessively enlarged, whereas the production of consumer goods and services is grossly underdeveloped. Estimation of redundant capacity varies from a quarter to a third of the gross industrial output; the economy is characterized by low technology and the downright waste of resources, which has brought about an ecological crisis. While the economy depends heavily on imports, its export potential lacks diversification.

Thus the main objectives of structural policy for today emerge as follows: to redistribute resources, with an emphasis on the consumer-goods sector of the economy, to upgrade technology dramatically, and to create sources for long-term growth.

We consider unacceptable those projects for which structural plans were made prior to the introduction of market institutions and which were guaranteed a place within the framework of the traditional (administrative) management infrastructure - the futility of such action has been proven by the whole experience of the Soviet economy. On the other hand, the distortions in the economy are so grave that they cannot possibly be dealt with by market mechanisms alone. State regulation of the economic infrastructure and investment appears necessary here.

The aims and mechanisms of the structural reorganization for the near, mid, and long run differ from each other in many respects.

In the coming one and a half years, that is, during the transition period, we will rely only on idle redundant capacities and available production resources, which are not being used effectively now, but will be exploited in the future.

By the end of the mid-term period, market institutions should be established and the economy should be structurally balanced.

A fundamental updating of technology, and the transition to a technologically intensive, ecology-conscious type of growth are objectives of a long-term perspective.

The program of transition to market relations treats the peculiarities of structural policy for the next year and a half. The key problem in the short run, connected with the orientation of economic stabilization and the hardening of credit and money policy, is to get a quick, "natural flow" response from the national economy to operations in the financial system.

It is impossible to create in a year and a half new major sources of goods supply. It is necessary to influence demand — to limit it dramatically — and simultaneously to stimulate the use of untapped resources, reserves, and waste.

A reduction of monetary stimulated demand will be achieved through the reduction of excessive state expenses, nonefficient production, and the swollen areas in the economy. Such reduction will be enacted from the very first day of the reform, at first with the help of administrative and management decisions. Primarily it will deal with the following areas of the national economy:

1. The military-industrial complex.
2. The investment sphere.
3. Hydro-electric construction, traditional forms of geological prospecting, routine maintenance and major repair of obsolete equipment, other areas with ineffective utilization of resources.
4. Ecologically hazardous production and basic industries —as demand for its products goes down.

To eliminate fictitious demand and a part of the redundant capacity, state purchases of some kinds of machinery (primarily military) will be cut down, centralized capital investment will be reduced, and budget subsidies to the unprofitable enterprises will gradually be taken away simultaneously with the development of market institutions. In this way the budget will shed a considerable sum of expenditures; conditions necessary to stabilize monetary circulation and many material, energy, and other resources will be released through a reduction of demand by their traditional consumers.

A reduction of the purchases of armaments and military equipment, a reorientation of defense enterprises to production of civilian consumer goods will take place, with a new conversion program in the defense industry.

The balancing of investment demand, by the government and the enterprises, has an equal importance for both the short and long term goals of structural policy, which correlates this demand with the resource capacities of the investment complex.

The new investment policy should, at its core, discern that a major part of current industrial construction is absolutely not justified either from the perspective of ultimate economic demand, or from the perspective of the efficient use of resources. Large-scale industrial construction is not backed by adequate resources and construction capacity, which results in construction taking two to three times longer than anticipated. Lack of labor and materials for the projects under construction results directly in the multimillion ruble waste of national resources. Moreover, the very structure of the plant still under construction demands expansion of raw material production.

Under these conditions, a drastic reduction in the number of projects under construction and the amount of capital investment in production will undoubtedly be beneficial if we consider redistributing a part of these resources to social programs.

It must be considered that different fields of production have different adaptation capabilities for development in the context of reduced investment. Besides, it is necessary to take into account the considerable differences in technological levels among investment projects.

A dramatic reduction in the ineffective management of capital investment and a simultaneous concentration of resources and efforts in those areas which give maximum return and meet the task of social reorientation of the economy should be considered first. Analysis shows that capital investments in production can be reduced or stabilized to a certain level:

a) **in metallurgy** - reduced demand for mass types of metallurgical products in connection with a reduction of industrial investments, transference of high-quality metals and alloys from the defense sector to the civilian sector, and the increased use of scrap iron released by higher rates of depreciation, can reduce investment needs by 15 to 20 percent as opposed to the level of 1986-1990;

b) **in the agricultural industry** - closing down without compensation of a considerable amount of livestock farms and reducing usage of low-quality and expensive agricultural machine supplies can dramatically reduce capital investment to tolerable levels. The volume of industrial capital investment in agriculture can be limited while investment in the light and food industries should rise by more than 30 percent;

c) **in the machine-building industry** - structural shifts in the end products of the civilian machine-building industry (developed in cooperation with the defense industry) made in favor of consumer goods products, direct reorientation of the fixed assets of the defense industry to civilian products and the cancellation of new construction of general machine-building projects, can reduce the volume of investment to 75 to 85 percent of the 1986-1990 level;

d) **in the construction industry** - as a result of a drastic shift away from high-rise housing, and as a result of large-scale application of locally produced materials for nonindustrial construction reducing the demand for traditional construction equipment, and with higher use of modern construction materials and better building design, and switching over to more reconstruction and reequipment, the rate of investment in construction can be preserved at its current level;

e) **in the transport and communication industry** - abandoning of new interregional railroad construction, the building of more spur tracks, more overpasses and junctions, an increase in the capacity of secondary tracks, settling the problem of rolling stock with a simultaneous drastic reduction in the need for trunk lines, and the preservation in general of current capital investment in the industry, an increase by 20 to 30 percent in investment for the development of local automobile roads and for aviation and sea transport, an increase by 60 to 80 percent in investment for communications and also for trade and material and technical supplies.

The situation calls for immediate structural changes. The reduction of ineffective industrial capital investment must be done right away, in one cut, within a year. An estimated reasonable reduction in industrial capital investment, taking into consideration the quality of investment and the real need for it, is 20 to 30 percent.

Simultaneously, as a result of such policy, demand for equipment will also go down by 15 to 20 percent. In this way the situation will become easier for investment in machine-building. This will mean, first, the creation of reserve capacities in machine-building; second, the creation of conditions for technological perestroika and an upgrading of machine-building products; and, third, the possibility for the reorientation of inefficient production to manufacture the things that are really needed.

The primary momentum, guaranteeing the reduction of industrial capital investment, must be provided by a number of strict administrative decisions to begin on October 1, 1990.
They are as follows:

1. To eliminate all the existing investment programs since they do not meet the real requirements of the national economy, to cut down special-purpose capital investment in production and military construction by no less than 30 percent.

2. To make an inventory, on the basis of independent expertise, of state enterprises already under construction in order to decide whether it is worthwhile to continue their construction. The criteria for the inventory includes the enterprises' social value, technological level, and planned terms of construction (these terms should be reduced preliminarily anyway).

    Upon completion of such inventory no less than 60 percent of industrial construction should be laid up. Beginning in November 1990, we should begin to sell sites of incomplete construction and loose pieces of equipment and material resources, possibly to foreign investors. In order to speed up this enterprise, we should use the results of the inventory made by Gosstroi USSR in 1990.

3. To limit demand for noncentralized investment we should raise interest rates for credit beginning in October 1990, and consider transition to free (negotiated) prices on construction products. During the economic stabilization period the maximum term for construction can be set at two years. Favorable tax and credit terms will be given to nonstate investors, and also to the contractors who build social and cultural projects.

4. Demonopolization of construction: in November 1990 all the general construction ministries are to be closed down and territorial associations and trusts are to be split into smaller units. These units currently control up to 60 to 70 percent of the contract market and construction materials. Construction organizations shall be provided with extra-territorial status and independence from the local authorities. The current banking system, which grants investment credits, will also be demonopolized; the dictatorial rights of the head design institutions will also be abolished.

Radical changes should happen not only in the process of establishing new funds and capacities (investment policy), but probably to a larger degree, in the functioning and reproduction of the existing industrial potential of the national economy (the policy of upgrading fixed assets). Liquidating the centralized assets of the ministries, cutting subsidies to unprofitable enterprises and imposing higher interest rates for credit will create grave financial difficulties for many enterprises. The government's demand for a number of products will go down. The reduction of redundant capacities under these conditions will happen through a drastic increase in asset liquidation (up to 5 percent per year in 1991-1995) and the termination (up to 20 percent) of the least effective part of the industrial bureaucracy without compensation.

At the same time, a profound structural maneuver being carried out in such a short time can result in grave negative aftereffects, such as:

- "bottlenecks" in the production infrastructure will limit possibilities to redistribute resources;
- termination of some production will damage certain technological chains;
- a considerable part of liberated resources will not be put to any use;
- a part of the research, technological, and skill potential of the economy will be lost.

In order to arrest these and other negative processes it is necessary to foresee and control structural changes, and also to take a number of special measures.

Primarily, market institutions will develop at a higher rate, especially the infrastructure for the redistribution of labor and material resources. As early as September 1990 the system of job placement and retraining of personnel will be reorganized; its staff will be retrained and equipped with special technology. Special programs will be developed for the areas where an especially high level of unemployment is expected. In certain cases, employees will be paid at full salary, even when an industry is closed. Information about the liberated material resources will go into the data banks of commercial brokers through which redundant equipment, materials, and waste shall be sold.

Secondly, a part of the released financial capital and material resources will go into dealing with the "bottlenecks" in the structure of the national economy (the production of building materials, new models of agricultural technology; the development of the social and industrial infrastructure) and to support reorganized enterprises (the conversion fund, the program of assistance to certain areas).

Third, the negative aftereffects of the structural changes will be cushioned with the help of facilities, raw materials, and energy reserves — both existing and newly created through the closing down of surplus facilities. During the transition period, imported supplies become especially important as the fastest way to fill gaps in the technological chain.

In dealing with the tasks of rapid structural change, we should not forget about long-term prospects for economic growth. That is why, having started the reform and upon getting reliable information about the state of the economy, it is necessary to develop, within six months, a concept and then a program of long-term structural changes

While closing surplus facilities, special attention will be paid to the preservation of potential long-term economic growth, and, primarily:

- the export industries;
- the scientific and technological potential of the defense complex;
- the intellectual potential of the country;
- the natural environment and recreational potential.

2

Conversion

Demilitarization of the national economy, employment of its accumulated industrial might, and mobilization of its military-industrial potential, covering both the industries of the defense complex and civilian industries which have military contracts, is a most important direction for the structural perestroika of the economy.

The conversion of the defense industry is aimed at the following:

- to bring down state expenditures by the reduction of military programs;
- to raise the technological level of civilian production by transferring advanced technologies, "know-how" and higher quality types of raw materials;
- redistribution of material and labor resources from the military to the civilian sector of the economy;
- closing a part of surplus facilities and, vice versa, increasing the output of civilian products by the enterprises of the defense industry;
- activation of new, advanced-technology-oriented sources of export.

Under conditions of strict financial limitations a program for full-scale conversion of the defense industry has poor prospects if we expect a quick return from the alternative use in the economy of the industrial and research basis of the defense sector.

In this situation, which is unfavorable for major investment programs, in the next year and a half we can rely only upon slow, inexpensive variants of transferring resources from the military to civilian production.

More capital-intensive variants are to come at later stages of the reform as a part of a policy of broad commercialization of the enterprises of the defense complex and involving foreign investors. An intermediate task for the near future is to screen and preserve potential sources of long-term growth. **In the long run the conversion is supposed to create** modern industries with high levels of technology, a powerful design and experimental base engaged in designing and producing military equipment and high-quality, durable consumer products. Preserving their military specifics, these enterprises must also become economically independent and develop the basis for long-term growth in the future market economy.

Over the next two to three years a considerable economic effect can be reached through:

1. Releasing raw materials and fuel stocks (with the newly established norms of reserves) to the civilian sector, switching over a part of the most mobile resources to nonmilitary orders;
2. Redistribution of those industrial facilities most capable of easily switching over to civilian orders;
3. Transferring a part of the released working force to vacant jobs in the civilian sector of the economy if their occupation and professional training permits it;
4. Switching the more flexible organizations in the research and development complex over to civilian projects.

FORMS OF CONVERSION FOR DEFENSE ENTERPRISES

1. **The search for new markets** (including export) will be expedient if an industry is equipped with unique and expensive machines which cannot be used for other purposes.

Technological rigidity and the absence of alternative consumers here is likely to be aggravated by the absence of reliable prospects in the domestic market, because of high prices for the product. These difficulties are counterbalanced by the modernization of technology aimed at lower production costs and lower product prices or at finding markets oriented to high-priced, high-quality products, though this is a rather expensive option.

2. **The maintenance of released facilities** is expedient in the case where there is not enough financing for profound modernization or reorientation of an enterprise, but it has considerable economic potential.

A specific form of "active maintenance" is to close down final assembly in a technological sequence responsible for mass production while preserving financial support for research and development (possibly preserving their defense orientation). This form has a serious drawback: it does not allow an immediate return from the reduction of military production.

3. A form of passive maintenance is **the transfer of material and equipment** that have become obsolete or redundant (e.g., navy vessels).

The difficulties of employing scrap in this country at this point can be compensated by selling it abroad. Some released resources, specifically, chemical weapons stocks, are due for destruction, which will require considerable investment for building the necessary facilities.

4. **Newly built and renovated industries** in this period of material and financial chaos and general decline in production find themselves in utterly unfavorable conditions and lack of investment is the primary reason for that.

Among the defense industries (shipbuilding, aircraft building, rocket production) there are only three branches - radio and telecommunication equipment, computer technology, and electric equipment - that have realistic chances to switch over to civilian markets in a short time (one to two years).

Other industries will take considerable time (five to seven years) to switch over to civilian products and considerable additional investment will have to be found for development possibilities in other fields. Thus the main effort at this point should go not only to transferring the more flexible types of military industry potential to the civilian sector, but also to a conservation of a part of the resources to maintain conditions for the realization of scientific and technological achievements.

WHAT IS NEEDED TO REALIZE THE SCIENTIFIC
AND TECHNOLOGICAL POTENTIAL
OF THE DEFENSE COMPLEX

1. **Patent protection and a survey of new inventions, a new policy for declassifying information.**

This action is necessitated by the lack of correspondence between Soviet law and a number of international patent and copyright laws; a great number of unpatented inventions which have considerable commercial potential; the illegal character of many technical borrowings, which deprives technologies for production and their products of their patent validity; unreasonable secrecy involving many inventions, applicable to civilian industry.

The function of checking the patent validity of products (technologies), when they are used outside the defense sector, and the technical and economic estimation of the equipment of enterprises under conversion should go to the service for interdepartmental expertise in the defense industry.

The use of the innovation potential of the defense complex will create the best chance to overcome the structural crisis in civilian machine-building in this country. This innovation potential includes design potential, experimental services connected with new production preparation, equipment, accessories, technologically intensive finishing operations, methods of technological control, etc.

In terms of involving foreign capital the following directions are the most promising:

- to use the powerful potential of the isotopes industry of Minatomenergoprom to produce extra pure materials, primarily for electronics (silicon, gallium arsenide), optoelectronics, and for other electrotechnologies;
- to reorient the technological potential of rocket production and radio-chemistry to the development of science-intensive low-tonnage chemistry (catalysts, activators, plasticizers, etc.);
- to use the machine-building potential of atomic and space technology to create a wide range of diagnostic instruments and technological equipment for the chemical industry;
- to cooperate on a large scale in the production of civilian aircraft on the basis of domestically produced designs of airframes with the engines, and the steering and navigation systems meeting international requirements;
- to use composites and a wide set of hardening and protective coatings for the most important parts of machines (primarily for engines), which should ensure frequent improvement of reliability of the whole apparatus;
- research in the field of laser employment in civilian systems; nonconventional sources of energy.

For a more accurate definition of the list of promising directions of foreign capital employment, independent experts from foreign consulting firms will be required.

2. **To withdraw defense enterprises from the respective ministries, to grant them complete economic independence, including the right to operate on the world market.**

No more than 20 to 30 percent of defense enterprises should remain under direct control of the state. These should be the enterprises with significant specialization in armaments and military equipment needed to maintain the current defenses of the country.

The mechanism of withdrawing enterprises from the military-industrial complex will be based on the denationalization of property, transforming them into stock companies and joint ventures.

The withdrawal of a considerable part of defense capacity from the military-industrial complex will allow the creation of a number of independent concerns with the following orientation:

- a metallurgical concern, specializing in high-quality steels, alloys, and the machine-building technologies for their processing based on existing enterprises of the Ministry of Defense;
- a concern to provide technological preparation for heavy-industry production (boring and mining equipment, axles for railroad platforms, heavy punches, etc.) based on artillery-weapons enterprises;
- a diversified network of small enterprises and companies based on the plants producing rifles; these would specialize in high-production automatic punches, small-sized mass production equipment and tools for rendering technological services (precision casting for the mass production of parts, the manufacture of special customized orders, and components for consumer goods, etc);
- several big concerns and a network of small enterprises connected with them to produce a wide variety of instruments for industrial and ecological purposes, parts for consumer goods, etc., and also machine-tool-building concerns, concerns for electrotechnical equipment and parts.

Research and production centers and design bureaus in research-intensive fields of the defense industry capable of producing multipurpose products (electronics, aircraft building, communication equipment, computers, lasers) can be switched over to civilian production right away.

Outstanding among the measures for defense industry conversion is the creation of a new technological base for the electronics industry to upgrade quality and bring down the price. These concerns can be built on the basis of the enterprises of Minatomenergoprom, Minelectronprom, and Minradioprom, involving also foreign partners. There should be no mass manufacturing of products that are not competitive on the world market. The employment of industrial isotope technologies and top-quality diagnostic instruments will dramatically increase the production of adequate electronic products, upgrade the quality, and bring down the costs.

The involvement of the Minatomenergoprom enterprises will play a decisive role in making electronic products competitive. A 30 percent reduction in nuclear armaments and the environmental problems of nuclear power engineering has undermined the concept of development for this ministry, which used to rely upon the further development and mass production of nuclear and thermonuclear weapons and the nominal effectiveness of nuclear and thermonuclear-power engineering. On the other hand, Minatomenergoprom possesses stocks of polymetallic ores which contain all the elements necessary for electronics; it also possesses available technologies, skilled personnel, and certain work already done for the isotope industry capable of swiftly increasing the production of pure and ultrapure materials (in accordance with world standards of purity); it also has the most modern control and measuring instruments and special equipment.

3. **The development of a domestic market for state of the art products** has key importance for tapping the scientific and technological potential of the defense industry. Without a drastic enlargement and modernization of reliable services for reception, relay, and also a network of terminals (radiotelephones, etc.), the use of the satellite communications system, which already exists in this country, is inconceivable. Being a rather expensive variant on the commercialization of the scientific and technological potential of the defense sector, the preparation of the market should proceed on the possibility of attracting foreign capital and in some cases priority should be given to initial orientation to existing markets in the West.

4. **The adoption of a new defense concept in the USSR** changes the content of the concept of "mobilization readiness of the defense industry." The existing mobilization potential is, technically, rigidly determined and oriented to the mass production of already developed types of weapons and military equipment. Along with the defense industries a wide range of civilian industries include special reserve facilities for this purpose.

The extraordinary modification of the technological infrastructure of all industries in the national economy, based on the built-in potential for dramatic increase in military production in the event of emergency, is one of the most important elements, though not obvious, of their mobilization potential.

At present because of the rigid plans and purpose behind the development and production of armaments and military technology, first, no possibility appears for later using the results of completed research in alternative areas, and, second, the building of this narrowly specialized potential has additional expense requirements, which will further impede conversion to civilian production. Thus (and also because of rigorous secrecy restrictions) the development of new types of scientifically intensive weapons does not lead to any increase in the technological level of civilian industries.

It is impossible to extrapolate the obsolete concept of mobilization potential and have it remain in harmony with modern defense objectives. The rates of the technological perfection of weapons are such nowadays that a quantitative increase of the existing military equipment cannot make up for the possible use of new types of weapons by an enemy.

The essence of a modern mobilization potential lies in the ability of the civilian economy to develop in event of emergency, on the basis of dual-purpose technology, mass production of diversified military equipment which is not in the army yet.

Such a concept does not require any mobilization potential in the conventional meaning - as a reserve of industrial and energetic capacities, preserved special equipment, special stocks of materials, etc. — ready for a large-scale production of armaments. Maintaining such a mobilization potential, not integrated into the market economy, would constantly require excessive treasury expenditures. The existence of this potential is profitable neither from the military nor from the economic point of view.

ORGANIZATIONAL AND LEGAL SUPPORT
FOR CONVERSION

In October and November of 1990 legal and normative acts are to be adopted which will regulate the process of reducing military orders, the reorientation and preservation of defense production, and the assistance of those areas which are adversely affected by the termination of military enterprises and projects.

Certain deadlines for prior notification of cancellation of orders are to be established as well as the time and terms of applying for assistance. The policy of secrecy in the defense sector is being reviewed. A stabilization fund for conversion is being created.

Indirect incentives and nongovernmental investments in particular are envisaged to stimulate the alternative use of military installations and plants.

Methods used to indirectly regulate the process of production reorientation are as follows:

- favorable rates of taxation of profits on civilian goods made at defense plants;
- benefits obtained from long-term credits to plants undergoing conversion;
- granting the right to accelerated amortization of fixed production assets;
- beneficial taxation of profit gained from the export of finished products;
- beneficial taxation of profits from collectives and organizations working in research and development in the defense sector when their developments are applied in civilian production.

Reorganization of defense plants is carried out at the expense of the conversion fund and under its control. Workshops with unique equipment may not be dismantled but should be mothballed based on the interdepartmental expert council's recommendation.

We must pay special attention to those who will lose their jobs due to the conversion or closing of defense plants, and employment must be found for them. Programs will be implemented to help people living in those regions most affected by a decrease of military orders.

3

The Construction Industry's Transition to Market Relations

Transition to market relations in the investment complex has to be carried out at an accelerated rate in order to take advantage of the low-technology monopoly in construction production and in order to rapidly eliminate its organizational monopoly, and to create high structural mobility and responsiveness to economic methods of management. Intensification of the market will overcome the crisis in capital construction and raise its role in the structural reconstruction of the national economy.

The construction industry is ready for the market in the following ways:

a) there are alternative arrangements of building organizations. In construction, as of January 1, 1990, the number of people working at cooperatives amounted to 16 percent of the total number of employees. About 5.7 percent of the employees were working in leased enterprises;

b) in a distorted market there are considerable barter operations for materials and contract work with a broad network of intermediaries;

c) the high criminal potential of this branch of economy results from the "paramarket" methods of management developed by industry leaders.

The most important precondition of a developed market for equipment, construction materials, projects, and contract work is a considerable slump in the demand for investments due to a sharp decrease in government budget expenditures and even the curtailment of a large portion of uncompleted construction.

The financing of capital investment will increase as early as the fourth quarter of 1990 and demand for investment will remain suppressed for 10 to 12 months because of a tough credit and financial policy.

The formation of market relations in the investment complex will follow three main routes.

First — Decentralization of investment sources for capital construction, deconcentration of all investment resources now in the hands of the state, and from the administrative method of their distribution among the industries and regions. The process, which began in 1987-1989, will enter into a qualitatively new phase.

In 1991 the following sources of financing capital construction will exist in the country:

- assets of the Union budget
- assets of the republican budgets
- assets of local budgets
- assets of enterprises and organizations
- assets of the population
- assets of foreign capital

A general slump in demand for investment will be accompanied by its redistribution to the benefit of the individual sphere of the economy and the nongovernmental sources of its financing.

As for groups of investors the situation will change in the following way:

1. **The Union budgets.** Centralized investments will actually make up not more than 15 percent of the total volume of demand. The new budget will cut the majority of expenditure items, including the rather unstable and growing social spending.

   The role of the Union budget for investing will decrease. New construction sites will be limited by the need to deal with the effects of technological and ecological disasters such as Chernobyl.

2. **The republican budgets.** The share of different republics in investment demand will vary from 15 to 35 percent. Economic sovereignty, mutual confrontations, and changes will lessen the possibility for surplus in the republican budgets. People's impatience with ecological problems in their region will increase the burden, yet improving the situation will involve new construction and considerable investments.

3. **The assets of enterprises and organizations.**

a) **Industrial enterprises**, associations, and economic organizations represent a large group of investors. Despite the fact that their share of investment demand has grown rapidly over the last few years, one should not expect this to continue under market conditions and for several reasons. Firstly, with the traditional absence of wholesale trade, a part of the noncash assets which client enterprises have in their funds for production development were artificially rechannelled to work on a contractual basis. The market for the means of production can more than recoup these assets, through the growth in prices for industrial and technical output. Secondly, downscaling of the state sector under the economic decentralization will mean that investors will change their attitudes toward expenses.

This implies that a structural crisis is a form of spontaneous reestablishment of distorted economic proportions at their lowest extreme. A rechannelling of resources into the agrarian sector may launch an investment boom in rural communities both in industrial and nonindustrial construction. Thus, in any case, the agrarian sector will acquire a high investment potential.

b) **The agricultural sector**'s growing role as an investor will not be connected to its current unfulfilled investment demand but with its future position. This will happen when the combination of the structural crisis and the transition to a market economy creates the appropriate conditions for a realistic redistribution of labor, materials, and financial resources. The root cause of this tendency is that the structural crisis is a form of a spontaneous resurrection of violated economic proportions which are now at their worst. The redistribution of resources in the agricultural sector can serve as the catalyst to an investment boom of construction in the production and nonproduction sectors in villages. In such a way, the agricultural sector will, in any case, possess high investment potential.

4. **Local budgets.** Decentralization of management objectively increases the role of the executive committees of the local soviets, and the recent legislative acts have strengthened their financial basis. We should also be mindful of the fact that the growing real power of the executive committees gives them more opportunities to influence the social, and economic policies of economic organizations and to participate in the development of the regional social infrastructures. As sectoral ministries are abolished, enterprises will sense a growing

need for various forms of support by local government. Finally, increasing social tensions, caused by the economic crisis, will put additional pressure on the local soviets to search for independent solutions to various social and economic problems in their regions. This provides grounds to believe that the executive committees of the local soviets will be active customers in the contract market for housing, social and public facilities, and other types of construction under programs which create new jobs.

5. **The population.** Command administration invariably discriminated against the population as a group of investors in the insufficiently developed market for housing and the shadow redistribution of resources for individual construction. Transition to a market economy will boost the role of individual investment. On the other hand, the growth of entrepreneurial opportunities will fulfill people's potential and increase their profits. Such profits will be channelled partly into investment in production, partly into housing construction. The latter will be promoted by housing reform. On the other hand, the expected transition of labor, material, and financial resources into the agrarian sector will create conditions for an accelerated development of social and individual housing construction. Besides, the need to move people from the Chernobyl area and mass migration from the sites of ethnic conflicts will also affect the volume of people's investments.

6. **Foreign capital.** The investment activity of foreign companies is greatly influenced by the lack of legislation and the unstable situation in this country. But already joint ventures are generating orders for construction through refurbishment of office space and hotels and small-scale production.

Transition to a market economy will give rise to new groups of investors, nonexistent today, such as investment banks and companies, international consortiums. Shareholders' organizations will be set up to commission housing construction with the aim of its further sale or lease. With a considerable growth in the current working capital in construction organizations, they will be able to carry out construction without specified customers and independently sell their constructed projects. However, we should not expect this investment demand to arise in the near future. These forms and areas of investment activity will take shape in 1993-1994 at best.

In 1990-1991 excessive investment demand will be suppressed not only through a tough budget and credit policy, but also through free market prices for construction. This will automatically make a tax on investment unnecessary and the probable index of the growth of construction prices will constitute 1.3 percent in 1991 and 1.95 percent in 1992. This is according to the Main Computer Center of the USSR State Planning Committee. Distribution of investments may be regulated by interest rates.

A system of regulated and listed prices for construction will be rendered inefficient in any case by barter operations, already widespread today.

One change in the relation between different sources of capital for investments is a structural shift toward nonindustrial services. Such shifts will occur in manufactured building supplies, structures, products, and the equipment delivered to construction sites. This will increase demand for cut wood, carpenter's products, plumbing equipment, glass, heat-retaining materials, ceramic tile, wallpaper, linoleum, paint and varnish products, pipes, gas and electric stoves, lifts, low-voltage equipment, cable and electrotechnical products. There could be an increase in orders for refrigeration, oxygen and special medical equipment for healthcare, construction of commercial and public catering facilities. At the same time the demand for various types of industrial construction supplies will fall. A major shift in the types of manufactured products takes time, huge capital investments in the refurbishment of the enterprises manufacturing building supplies, and considerable changes in the structure of economic ties and in the context of the distribution of resources. This plan, the difficult transition to market relations, is, however, impossible without it.

- Republics and local soviets should consider granting funds and credits on preferential terms for:
- extending the production of building supplies and related equipment in this country;
- enterprises' purchases abroad of these materials;
- purchasing plants abroad to manufacture these products, with money allocated by organizations and local soviets.

Problems of adaptation will apply to the organization of production and management, the system of production and technical equipment delivery, the structure of construction organizations, relations with subcontractors and many other issues. The adaptation process for construction organizations currently specializing in industrial construction will require major internal restructuring and the resolution of enormous material, financial, organizational, social, and sociopsychological problems. In doing so, they will have to immediately enter into competition in the augmented and reduced contract market with the construction organizations with extensive experience in the nonproduction sphere.

The second area for establishing market relations in construction is to eliminate the administrative subordination of customers and contractors and to extend the market for contractual work, **switch to a system of "contract bargaining."**

This will not lift the limitations on concluding contractual agreements. Government regulation will focus on:

- organizing the contract bidding to be held by the state committees on construction of the USSR and the constituent republican state orders;
- setting up independent firms of government certified experts to examine the quality of projects and construction and to make recommendations on concluding contractual agreements and insuring constructed projects and to assess risks and perform other insurance operations;
- establishing a governmental and independent agency for licensing construction organizations and holding contract bidding;
- reorienting the state committees on construction of the USSR and the constituent republics toward the elaboration of common standards, similar to standards in European countries for construction, architecture, city planning, recommended norms, prices, etc., and prognostication of construction development. Contract bidding may be public or closed. Public bidding is in fact the same as a stock exchange where a customer's demand is balanced against a contractor's supply. When technically complicated projects are constructed, closed bidding is preferable. In this case, a customer sends out individual inquiries to construction companies of his choice to participate in the bidding. The customer informs them of the most important aspects of the contract (type, scale of construction, required time frame, and terms of construction). If there is a ready project plan, interested companies can look through it and then submit their proposals on the terms of the contract to the customer within the agreed period of time. The customer considers them and compares them with the proposals from other potential contractors based on the costs and terms of the contract, possible improvements of the project's additional conditions and guarantees. As a result, a contract is signed.

State orders for construction are introduced only for the duration of the transition period and are backed by tax privileges or subsidies to the customer (general contractor) from the Union, republican, or local budget.

The third trend in promoting market relations is *decentralizing* management, creating versatile forms of property, and demonopolizing of economic activity in construction.

The policy which set up the major organizational structures (designing and construction, designing and industrial construction, and other such types), adopted at the beginning of the present five-year-plan, has been upstaged by a tendency toward smaller organizational structures arising from the pattern of economic change.

Many construction agencies are now considering leaving the trusts and associations which they believe to be useless superstructures.

If it allows agencies to quit, a trust can grow into an engineering and management firm, strengthen its engineering services and independently enter the contract market. In this situation it may work with its former member-agencies on a subcontract basis to avoid the current economic conflicts. Moreover, the trust would organize subcontract bidding, inviting its former agencies as well as agencies of other trusts, cooperatives, leaseholding and other construction organizations.

When construction market conditions sharply deteriorate, the trusts will get interested in this line of evolution, as they will be unable to provide work for all their member-agencies and to subsidize the weakest. On the other hand, with poor market conditions the agencies may cling to trust structures as guarantors of their economic security.

Territorial construction associations are also facing major evolution. Most of them, together with all their subordinate nonproductive organizations, have to create a foundation in the emerging market infrastructure for the construction organizations of the region. The market infrastructure of a region may include commercial banks; commodity exchanges; wholesale firms; engineering, consulting, and development companies; leasing agencies; auditing, factoring, and service organizations; and so on. All of them must act as legal entities, performing concrete jobs, carrying out orders, offering their services in contracts with construction organizations.

Organizing contract bidding may become another function for a specialized firm upon its withdrawal from a construction trust.

The infrastructure of the labor market in construction must develop at priority rates if investment demand is rapidly falling. Lower demand for personnel at construction organizations may be offset by quick reorientation toward nonindustrial construction and by partly reducing the volume of construction. Some of the redundant workers will go to construction cooperatives. We should concentrate on searching for foreign orders for specialized construction organizations. Special emphasis will be placed on the regions of recent major construction (Western Tyumen, Yamal, Baikal-Amur Railway, etc.).

While reducing the scope of investments and demonopolizing the construction industry, we should preserve the technical and labor potential which will allow us to start increasing investments in one and a half to two years. However, it is possible to curb our tendency to put key assets into operation by concentrating all resources on a limited number of essential capital construction projects.

4

Development of the Industrial Infrastructure

Transition to a market economy will make higher demands on the industrial infrastructure — transport, communications, logistics. If these sectors do not live up to potential demand, at least at the minimal level, then development of the market may be brought to a halt.

Meanwhile, the industrial infrastructure has been increasingly falling behind as of late. The year 1989 saw a decline in the freight turnover for all kinds of transport (except gas pipelines). Simultaneously, the length of transportation of one ton of cargo grew during one year by an amount equal to the total increase for the previous five years. The supplies at storehouses are growing, a measure of the slowed turnover of extremely scarce material resources. The economic losses caused by inadequate rail transportation alone are estimated at 1.2 billion rubles annually. According to estimates, the poor transportation system causes a total damage of 30-40 billion rubles a year.

This situation is mainly explained by the outdated material and technical base of the industrial infrastructure. The growth rates from 1971 to 1990 of essential production assets in transportation constituted only about 70 percent, and in railway transport 45 percent of the average of the economy. Even the allocated funds were used extremely irrationally, primarily on projects like the Baikal-Amur Railway, by not tackling the most urgent problems.

Finally the worst bottlenecks in the development of the industrial infrastructure were:

- an insufficient network of paved roads, particularly in the countryside, their unsatisfactory technical condition, and a lag in the automobile service base (garages, parking lots, repair shops, service stations);

- a lag in the development of railroad switch yards, the wear and tear on railway tracks, installations and rolling stock beyond the established limits, the lack and imperfection of loading mechanisms and track machines;
- insufficient capacities of seaports, which leads to overstocking and holds back the development of foreign economic operations; an obsolete fleet, in which the average service life of vessels in the transportation network is nearly 15 years (in 1989);
- in civil aviation the wear and tear of aircraft and engines is 60 percent. Aircraft maintenance facilities are about 55 to 60 percent equipped; the fleet is comprised of planes and helicopters that were built in the early 1970's.

Communications system data transfer is extremely backward and inhibits foreign investors from investing in the USSR.

Storage capacities for various types of agricultural produce are insufficient and irrational in their structure. In agriculture, large stockyards, storehouses, and grain elevators prevail, but they require long-distance transport during conditions of an acute shortage of small, technically equipped storehouses. The storage capacities for wholesale trade and supply are absolutely insufficient.

The state of water and heating supply systems, particularly in the cities where they are vital elements of the life-support system, causes concern.

All elements of the production infrastructure are working at full capacity but without reserves. However, for a market economy it is necessary to have reserve capacities at 25 to 35 percent levels. Otherwise, it is impossible to carry out urgent decentralization and demonopolization, to split up large automobile enterprises into smaller units, and to create a number of shipping and air companies on a shareholder basis. Contractual discipline is irrelevant without a supply of railroad cars and other similar factors.

This problem is intensified because under market conditions enterprises are initially unlikely to invest their resources in the physical infrastructure, preferring projects with quick returns. This is especially because a stringent financial credit policy, which will be unavoidable during the next two years, will create conditions for a contraction in capital investment.

It follows that the republics, The Union, and the local organs of power will have to take upon themselves the development of the productive infrastructure. In order to do this a special All-Union program will be necessary. It is necessary to attract not only the resources of all the governmental budgets but also business resources, population resources, and foreign investment to realize this program. This program should have high priority.

According to evaluations by the Academy of Sciences and other research institutes, the volume of capital investment in the productive infrastructure over the next several years can be maintained only with considerable increases in effectiveness, which includes changes in the investment patterns. With a decrease in the construction of train tracks and pipelines, it is important to put resources into increasing the capacity of loading stations and renewal of the pipeline facilities. Investment in local highways must be increased by 20 to 30 percent and investment in the distribution network for trade and supply must be increased by 60 to 70 percent.

In order to utilize the potential of motor vehicle, aviation, and marine transport, it is necessary to denationalize and demonopolize these industries. For example, the industrial carriers must be sold off to create a series of marine and airline companies that would be based on stock ownership. At the same time, railways and pipelines, the bulk of roads, the infrastructure of water transport and airports will remain the property of the state for the foreseeable future.

5

Land Reform and Agrarian Policy

The agrarian market is best prepared for the introduction of market relations. Small- and medium-sized enterprises, which are subject to privatization and price fluctuations, mitigate the effect of monopoly trends. More than a third of the food consumption of the population is already covered within the framework of the existing market (personal subsidiary plots, the collective-farm market, consumers' cooperatives). The correlation of profitability levels, prices, and the volumes of subsidies in the state sector is such that the introduction of a market will not substantially change the established proportions and networks. The output of produce is an exception because it has the largest volume of subsidy (meat, dairy products - 65 percent of all subsidized prices).

Subsidizing, which has become a difficult sociopolitical problem, seriously impedes the introduction of market relations in the agroindustrial complex.

In the agrarian sphere the main tasks during the transition period are:

- the introduction of market relations in all components of the agroindustrial complex, stabilization on the sale price of normal volumes of subsidized foodstuffs and the sale of additional volumes of products at free prices;
- land, and the denationalization of land and the basic assets of farms and enterprises of the agroindustrial complex;
- elimination of existing managerial structures and the transfer of their power to regulate agrarian relations to the local soviets;
- the elaboration and implementation of ad hoc programs for the development of the production and social infrastructure in the countryside.

FORMATION OF MARKET RELATIONS IN THE AGROINDUSTRIAL COMPLEX

Market relations in the agroindustrial complex are to be introduced to the fullest extent without any restrictions.

The formation of a commercial enterprise network engaged in wholesale trade will begin in October.

From January 1991 products of the agroindustrial complex will be sold through wholesale trade based on free price formation.

Government intervention in the supply of material resources to agriculture aims to overcome supplier monopoly, which includes control over prices, breaking up organizational monopolies into smaller units, and creating parallel structures. In the transition to wholesale trade in agricultural machine repair products, it is not expected that prices will substantially rise, since the profitability of this sector is sufficiently high, while the degree of saturation of agriculture with serially produced machines exceeds the real requirements.

Simultaneously a market for secondhand agricultural machines will be created. Specialized enterprises (former repair plants of the former Ministry of Auto and Agricultural Machinery of the USSR) will select, repair, and sell these machines, guaranteeing their reliability for a period of time.

Import deliveries will play a noticeable role in satisfying agriculture's needs for machines, particularly small ones. This will include special-purpose aid, the sale of secondhand machines at reduced prices, etc.

We believe that it is possible to avoid the introduction of a tax-in-kind in agriculture. The size of republican and Union food supplies are shrinking, while procurement of these supplies is made on the basis of state orders placed in accordance with the general principles of the contract system. Limited volume, contract prices, tax privileges, and possible two-way deliveries of products for material and technical purposes will help make the state order for agricultural products profitable for all types of agricultural enterprises and relieve administrative pressures. There will be severe economic sanctions for failure to accept or fulfill a state order, particularly in the first two years. In the present-day situation it is expedient to place state orders with large enterprises that have a high rate of profitability and a high ratio of commodity output to total output.

Outside the confines of the state order, enterprises have the right to determine for themselves the channels and volumes of the goods they produce. The system of fixing purchase prices and production volumes from the center is eliminated. Relations between agricultural enterprises and purchasing and processing enterprises are based on contracts.

In order to overcome the monopoly of the enterprises processing agricultural products, measures are to be taken to encourage the construction of small processing shops directly at the farms, including some which use complete sets of imported equipment. The amalgamation of district farms in order to purchase the basic assets of food-industry enterprises and the establishment of cooperatives, associations, and joint-stock companies for purchasing, transporting, processing, and selling agricultural produce is also encouraged.

Responding to the needs of retail trade are the purchasing and processing enterprises, which, by virtue of their material interests, will decide for themselves in each region the volume and the range of their purchases of agricultural produce.

While the number of markets in cities and towns will be considerably increased, a network of agricultural commodity exchanges and information banks will be created. The development of commercial purchasing activities in any form is encouraged.

The departure from the practice of administratively setting the volumes and range of agricultural produce will allow us in two to three years to substantially intensify farm specialization and reduce production costs. It will also stimulate interest in the proper selection of farm animals and crops and their distribution by regions.

Problems may arise during the transitional period due to changes in organizational structure and the size of cultivated areas. New mechanisms for price formation and commodity intervention by the state will eliminate overspecialization on farms.

Leading local bodies will organize working goals to form a new infrastructure for trade and encourage privatization and demonopolization in this sphere. Trade enterprises decide retail prices on the basis of aggregate costs of production, processing, and selling of agricultural produce, taking into consideration the supply-and-demand situation. In October 1990, work to privatize fruit and vegetable storage facilities in towns and cities will already be in progress. In this sphere organizational monopolies will be eliminated.

THE MECHANISM AND EXTENT OF SUBSIDIZING AGRICULTURAL PRODUCTION

Shifts in subsidies away from the purchasing and processing of agricultural produce and toward trade are based practically totally on local budgets, which have corresponding revenues to finance them. Depending on the specifics of their respective regions, the local soviets themselves establish the size and form of subsidies for commercial enterprises, with subsidies going only to the finished products to be sold through the retail trade system. All subsidies are fully eliminated from the intermediate stages. With this aim in mind a subsidy fund is set up on the basis of the redistribution of government budgetary subsidies and local tax revenue. In 1991 financial aid may be rendered to local authorities from their respective republic budgets to establish their subsidy funds. The subsidy fund of a local budget may also be accumulated from fines imposed for unjustified price increases or unfair competition, among other reasons.

The proposed mechanism may be introduced in most regions in the Soviet Union, with the exception of Moscow, Leningrad, Armenia, Azerbaijan, Georgia, and Turkmenia, where the consumption structure is marked by a large share of food imports, which falls outside the sphere of the budgetary subsidy mechanism. For this reason the transition period presupposes foreign exchange spending on food imports for the above-mentioned consumers in line with an agreement among all the republics. A special fund has been set up as part of the USSR food fund to support individual regions.

PRINCIPLES UNDERLYING THE FORMATION AND SIZES OF THE ALL-UNION AND REPUBLICAN INVENTORIES OF AGRICULTURAL PRODUCE

The federal agricultural produce inventory has been considerably reduced, primarily because of the elimination of the government-operated market inventories and the industrial processing inventories for mixed feed and forage. It incorporates the revised inventories for nonmarket consumption, export deliveries, and state reserves. The total size of the federal food inventory should not exceed 15 million tons of grain and 2 million tons of meat.

The state-run contract system makes purchases for the centralized federal inventory on the basis of generally established methods. The size and composition of state orders for produce deliveries to the federal food inventory are determined at the Union level by agreement among all the republics and are then proposed to the republic contract systems. Here the full size of state orders and the terms for placing them are finalized with due regard for relevant agreements and internal needs.

Later on, the federal food inventory may be reduced to the size of its reserve portion with the introduction of local supplies for the armed forces, the Ministry of Internal Affairs, the KGB, and other organizations through direct budgetary appropriations for these customers.

During the transition period in the republics, it is necessary to establish small reserve inventories on the functional lines of the federal inventory. Under specific circumstances the republican inventories may mediate some of the intrarepublic interregional procurement of food and other agricultural produce. The federal and republican inventories will be used for commodity interventions on the market and to assist those regions which have a poor supply of food.

A SYSTEM OF MEASURES TO STABILIZE
THE FOOD MARKET

In the context of unrestricted pricing the established proportions in consumption levels of foodstuffs may be violated because of the conflicting interests of local commercial-procurement organizations and agricultural producers. Such conflict may lead to smaller volumes of sales and higher prices.

The government's agrarian policy will seek to stabilize retail prices by:

- eliminating the monopoly of producers, processors, and commercial enterprises and promoting competition;
- saving on the aggregate costs of production of foodstuffs;
- increasing production and sharply reducing farm output losses;
- maintaining the guaranteed consumption level of staple foodstuffs at low state-fixed prices.

The monopoly status of procurement, processing, and trade enterprises should be phased out through early privatization, the all-out encouragement of trade and procurement cooperatives, and the priority development of the infrastructure of the food market. Large numbers of trucks (including military ones) will be sold to private citizens, and cooperatives will be set up to service them. Imports will include complete sets of equipment for small processing plants. A network to store farm produce will be developed on the farms themselves. Several dozen private farms will be established in the vicinity of big cities, using foreign technologies and enlisting the services of foreign experts to help train personnel. Every form of assistance on both the governmental and private levels will be accepted in the organization of agricultural production.

Aggregate costs of food production will be reduced by eliminating lump-sum allocations from the state budget for the construction of irrigation facilities, large cattle-breeding complexes, and giant plants for the processing and storage of produce. Direct food purchases from farmers and the owners of personal subsidiary plots will help do away with the artificially created gap in purchase prices between different categories of producers and will help reduce the general level of prices. The self-interest of the owners of the means of production and of output will promote a sharp reduction in losses, while government agencies will fight against unfair competition, the stockpiling of commodity surpluses, and other such occurrences.

There will be an increase in the production of certain types of farm produce even in the first and second years of the reform due to increased specialization on farms and improved organization of farming. However, stable and lasting growth of production will require investments in the selection and breeding business, the development of new types of agricultural machinery, and modernization of the processing industry.

Food imports remain a major factor for market stabilization during the transition period.

LAND REFORM

Land reform will create conditions for effective economic activity in diverse forms, eliminate the monopoly in land ownership, and introduce payment for use of land. The specific forms, the time limits, and the methods of transforming land-ownership relations (including questions of its sale and private ownership) will be determined by the sovereign republics while the local authorities will carry out the main organizational work to effect the reform.

On October 1, the President of the USSR will declare the inalienable right of the people to own land and confirm the local soviets' powers to use it. The lands belonging to collective and state farms will be declared to be the sum total of the allotments of their farm workers, and the reregistration of land will begin.

In 1990 the legal, organizational, and economic fundamentals of land reform will be completed. Republican land codes and direct-action legislative acts will be adopted which will regulate the collection of land taxes and payments for leaseholds on the land, the requisition and allocation of lands, the introduction of a land cadastre and land monitoring, and the terms of the sale of plots of land. The local soviets will approve the corresponding methodological and normative documents. At the same time, the obsolete legislative acts, instructions, and regulations, which contradict the fundamental legislation of the USSR and Union republics on land, will have been annulled.

Republican committees on land reform with extensive networks of local branches will be set up. Clear and coherent methods for carrying out all measures within the framework of land reform and privatization of fixed agricultural assets, with consideration for peculiarities of individual regions, will be worked out. Land-use consultancy, control and arbitration functions to implement the legislation on land reform adopted by the republics will be assigned to the committees on land reform. To neutralize the local sabotage of this legislation, changes in the civil and criminal law will be made.

Reregistration will be carried out by the local soviets in cooperation with the committees on land reform, taking the actual use of land into account. The local soviets will grant plots of land for ownership and use (including leasing) to agricultural enterprises, and for life-long ownership, with the right to bequeathal, to citizens.

Peasants will be granted the right to have plots of land. The land used for personal cultivation will be declared to be the personal property of a peasant family or will be turned over to it for a small payment. Tentative privatization of the land and fixed production assets — the registration of shares, stocks, etc. — will take place at the collective and state farms, taking into account local conditions. Peasants who wish to engage in joint economic activity will form cooperatives which carry full liability, or cooperatives and cartels with limited liability. The same procedure will be established for the state farms and interfarm agricultural enterprises. After the signing of the corresponding statutes and contracts, the soviets will register the new formations.

This legislation formalizes the right to voluntary withdrawal of a farm worker from a collective farm with a plot of land which becomes his property and with his share of accumulated property in-kind, or in the form of a security, yielding dividends. The procedure for reappraisal and the mechanism for withdrawing from a farm will be regulated by statute and contract.

The mechanism to grant plots of land may require citizens to submit their applications to the rural (settlement) Soviet of People's Deputies and to indicate the purpose for their use of this land, its size and location. If the plot of land is more than the land used by collective and state farms or other agricultural enterprises, decisions on this will be made after the respective deputy commission of the district Soviet of People's Deputies considers the issue.

If a farm and the withdrawing farm worker do not reach an agreement on a specific plot of land on which to organize a peasant farm, a reconciliation commission, composed of representatives of the deputy commission of the Soviet of People's Deputies, the rural (settlement) soviet, the farm, and the committee on land reform, will be appointed.

The reconciliation commission's recommendation serves as grounds for adoption of a final decision by the district Soviet of People's Deputies, the decisions of which may be appealed in court if, in the view of one of the parties, the law has been violated.

The district Soviet of People's Deputies will grant plots of land to other citizens, who do not work at the given enterprise, from its land in reserve. A period of probation (up to three years) may be established during which the land is used on a leasehold basis with its subsequent transfer to ownership.

The lands in reserve for the formation of peasant farms and small cooperatives will be enhanced by the addition of requisitioned lands of unprofitable or low-profit farms incapable of ensuring their effective use. There are about 6 million hectares of unutilized lands in the Non-Black-Soil Zone alone.

On the basis of their location it is necessary to work out plans for organizing the use of land. Such plans would envisage measures to formalize land ownership by peasant farms, collective and state farms, forestries, and other land users.

Following decisions about their work collectives, collective and state farms will be transformed into cooperatives of peasant farms and reorganized in different ways in different republics and regions. This can be done gradually. In the first stage, the system of participation for members of collective farms and workers on state farms in the profits of enterprises will be developed and mastered. The system of leasehold relations and other forms of farm production is encouraged. At the second stage, a collective or state farm will be transformed into a cooperative uniting producers and rendering comprehensive services to them.

Programs to support commodity peasant farms will be implemented in the republic. According to the preliminary estimates, taking into account the resource possibilities, there are plans to set up 150,000 to 180,000 peasant farms in the next few years. Their organization will be more intensive in the Non-Black-Soil Zone, some regions of Siberia, the Baltic Republics, the highlands and foothills of the Transcaucasus, and in the western Ukraine. According to forecasts, they will specialize in the production of milk, beef, sheep, pigs, and some crop farming. Crop farming will focus on the production of potatoes and vegetables in the open and on protected ground, and fruit, and in some zones, cereals and industrial crops, and ecologically clean products.

An estimated investment needed to set up the forecast number of peasant farms amounts to 13-30 billion rubles (150,000 to 200,000 rubles per farm).

State allocations, credits, and the money accumulated by the population will be the sources of financing.

According to the preliminary estimates, if the size of a peasant farm is 100 hectares for farms and other lands, then all peasant farms will occupy 15-18 million hectares. Starting in 1990, land banks will be set up in the republics. Their statutory capital is provided from budget funds (banks can be based on sections of the Agroprombank — Agricultural and Industrial Bank). The list of the functions of the land banks includes: long- and short-term crediting, acquisition of land as property, mortgages, underwriting and purchasing stocks and shares in cooperatives, and so on. Such a bank must operate strictly on a commercial basis in cooperation with state agencies. The state agrarian policy is to be pursued with the receipts from special-purpose subsidies and the introduction of taxation on favorable terms.

The introduction of payments for land is the most effective lever for land reform. In the course of the cadastral survey of the land stock, the preliminary cost of land is tentatively calculated and a land tax, which impels farmers to make effective use of the land, is introduced.

Effective forms of economic activity will be reorganized and land and other agricultural stocks will be released in the process of bankruptcy and liquidation of the collective and state farms which work at a loss. As of January 1, 1990, every sixth farm was classed as economically weak, 65 short-term credits had no material backing, and the deficit in the farms' circulation funds reached 38.4 billion rubles. Taking into account that 70 percent of the financial resources of collective and state farms consist of credits, an increase in the bank interest rate to 6 to 8 percent will lead to the bankruptcy of up to 25 percent of all farms, which will affect about 30 percent of farm lands, as of January 1, 1991.

Bankruptcies shall be dealt with as follows: declaration of insolvency, seizure of production assets, and their sale at open auctions. The depreciated value of unsold production assets shall be transferred to the account of the creditor's land bank. The bank shall then, jointly with the local soviet, declare a competition to purchase or lease the vacant agricultural land. Local residents shall be given preferential rights for the purchase of the land for sale. After examining submitted documents, the bank shall give loans or preferential credits for the purchase (or lease) of the land, and fixed and liquid assets.

The new owner of the land shall use his own or borrowed money to buy or lease machinery, construction materials, fertilizer, and so on, and sign contracts to sell future crops.

After the implementation of the basic provisions of the reform, the local soviets shall lose the right to own or dispose of land, except for the land in the state reserve. The soviets shall retain the control over proper use of land, conclude trading transactions on land, and perform other functions stipulated by the law.

Under the land reform, local authorities may sell, for modest prices, plots of land of up to 600 square meters in size to urban residents. The procedure for allotting land to gardening partnerships will change. They may now be given the cultivated land of unprofitable farms situated at least 30 to 50 kilometers outside the city boundaries. This will ensure a speedy rise in the production of potatoes, vegetables, fruit, and berries for the producers' consumption and sale. This measure is part of the government's social program and is expected to cushion the hardships in the transition period for millions of families.

The purchase of large sections of land and resettlement aimed at creating a farm shall be regulated by local soviets in accordance with the land law.

The pace of the land reform, and its specific forms shall be chosen with due account of local conditions and will vary considerably in different parts of the Union.

A NEW MECHANISM FOR THE PROGRAM OF SOCIAL AND ECONOMIC ASSISTANCE TO THE COUNTRYSIDE

Assistance to villages and farms should be an important and effective lever boosting the productivity of agriculture and related industries. However, the targets and forms of such help should be changed.

There should be no more free aid through subsidies and budget allocations. The practice of writing off the farms debts to banks should also be discontinued. Assistance shall be given only for repayment in money and shall be given only to those farms which can promise a growth in output.

Finances for target-oriented programs to develop the countryside's social and manufacturing infrastructure will be generated by reducing the centralized investment for irrigation, for creating large livestock complexes, plants, and storage facilities. Investment programs shall be financed by the land banks, the Union, republican or local budgets, the associations of producers, or the farmers themselves.

The republics may introduce incentives for peasant farms for the next few years. These may include:

- introducing tax benefits for peasant farms during the initial stage of their operation; no taxation on that part of the peasants' incomes which is spent on expanding production;
- promoting a special system of small crediting institutions in rural areas on a commercial and cooperative basis; instructing state-run banks to establish a preferential practice granting credit to peasant farms during the initial stage of their operation; providing benefits to those commercial crediting institutions which serve peasant farms;
- working out budget financing programs to create the infrastructure in those areas where peasant farms spring up en masse.

Targeted investment is intended to develop regional construction capacities, create new types of agricultural machinery and build roads.

In order to involve foreign partners in the effort to create peasant farms, it is necessary to work out a package of measures to enhance the interest of foreign firms and businessmen in investing their capital in the construction of production facilities, technical, technological, agricultural, and social services; in supplying high-grade seeds, technology, fertilizer, means of plant protection, and in instituting training and retraining courses.

6

Housing Reform

Housing reform is one of the key aspects of the transition to a market economy. Its purpose is to create a market for housing, which would allow any family or adult individual to choose the most appropriate way to improve living conditions.

The market should be a flexible instrument. It should give opportunities for all sections of the population to improve their living conditions and stimulate the construction of new housing and better use of existing premises.

The transition to a market in this sphere is necessitated by the great amount of unsatisfied solvent demand for housing. In existing estimates, such demand amounts to 70 to 75 billion rubles. Of this figure, 7 billion are already in the pockets of people on the cooperative waiting list and another 12 billion in the purses of those who are not on the waiting list for such apartments, but who would like to have them anyway. Ready money to build individual houses amounts to 25 billion rubles (without credits). Three and a half billion rubles have been saved by people wishing to reconstruct or refurbish the housing they have. The remaining sum of over 25 billion will be readily paid by people living in state-owned apartments who wish to improve their living conditions.

We should not ignore this tremendous solvent demand. At present, 50 percent of the money saved for housing is spent to buy other goods, which undermines the balance on the consumer market.

We suggest the following main principles for housing reform:

1) The right of every citizen and family to buy housing, legally own it, sell it, and bequeath it without any limitations.
2) The right of every citizen and family to freely choose their housing: a separate house in private possession, an apartment, a cooperative possession, or rental.

3) Housing should be fully paid for at the market value, with consideration for its quality and geographical location.
4) Low-income families should be given social guarantees. Their municipality or the state should allocate them housing free of charge from municipal housing funds.
5) People on official waiting lists for housing should receive preferential treatment.

The housing reform will have important social significance. It will turn the majority of citizens into owners. It will boost saving incentives, investment, and motivation.

The reform will also facilitate balancing the state budget. The state will no longer spend unreasonably huge amounts of resources for housing construction and maintenance. According to the previous program of expanding housing construction, the state was to dramatically increase investment. The money set aside for this investment, which is now withheld from the population and used to dole out apartments through the state distribution system, will be paid to the citizens, who will spend it without restrictions.

A majority of enterprises will discontinue shouldering the heavy financial burden of unfairly distributed expenses for housing construction and housing maintenance services.

Housing reform is envisaged to be effected in stages over the period from 1990 to 1992.

In the first stage (October 1990-March 1991) we will create the legal foundation and the socioeconomic structure of the housing market and start the privatization of certain categories of housing for a token payment.

In the second stage (up till the end of 1991) we will sell a part of newly built apartments for cash or on credit, restructure the credit system for housing construction, establish rules for providing housing to those who are eligible for housing based on the official lists and to low-income families. We will then prepare the next stage of reforms.

In the third stage (late 1991-1992) we will introduce payment for housing at its full market cost, with compensation to people through the adopted system of indexation. We will start large-scale privatization of state housing, transfer or sell departmental and enterprises' housing to the Soviets of People's Deputies, to people inhabiting the apartments, or to specialized commercial companies.

The brunt of the work involved in carrying out the housing reform will be borne by local soviets. Republican and central bodies will guarantee the legal status and the financial support for these measures.

Creation of the legal underpinning and the socioeconomic infrastructure of the housing market presupposes:

* the drafting and adoption of legal acts that will guarantee the free purchase, sale, or lease of the housing supply owned by the people at contract prices;
* the creation of conditions for the development of commercial companies that will buy, build, sell, and lease housing; the creation of departments concerned with the purchase and sale of the housing supply at executive councils of soviets; and the drafting of regulations on the procedure of buying and leasing housing from local soviets;
* the establishment of a system of specialized housing credits; the creation within the banking system of a mechanism for extending additional credit preferences to young and low-income people and large families; and
* the drafting and adoption of legal statutes on the restructuring of the system of cooperative housing along two main principles:
  a) the restructuring of the existing housing cooperatives into companies for joint maintenance of housing blocks during the privatization of apartments; and
  b) the creation of cooperatives to construct new apartment buildings, with subsequent private ownership of the apartments, or with preservation of the cooperative form of property, depending on the will of builders (buyers).

Free transfer of certain categories of apartments to dwellers or their sale at nominal prices is the first step toward the privatization of housing.

Dwellers will get free allotment of housing in accordance with norms determined by local soviets, paying for surplus floor space. It is possible that the housing will be sold at token prices. This sale, with 7 percent taxes on the depreciated cost or at 10 rubles per square meter, could bring the government 10-20 billion rubles, while families will pay 500-600 rubles for their apartments whose market price amounts to 10,000-30,000 rubles.

The privatization of housing will initiate mass apartment exchanges, that is, the sale and purchase of personal apartments, with the difference in the list price of the apartments paid by those who move into the better living quarters.

Local soviets can establish schedules for the transfer or the symbolic sale of apartments (for example, till July 1 or December 1, 1991). After that apartments will be sold and bought only at market prices.

Apartment exchanges will intensify noticeably because commercial brokerage in apartment exchanges will become legal, which will improve the
distribution of housing and, more importantly, reduce the demand for new
apartments, encourage the people to maintain housing in better condition,
reduce the burden on municipal transport due to a more reasonable distribution of the people in the city, and increase the mobility of the population.

The improvement of the process of transfer and purchase of housing and,
in general, its privatization depends on the restructuring of the system of rent
in state-owned apartment projects and public stock in accordance with the
rules established in the republics. They could adhere to the following
principles:

- to raise rent for surplus floor space as of October 1, 1990;
- to establish in 1991 different rents for one-family apartments, depending on the floor space, quality of housing and region, but not lower
  than exploitation costs;
- to provide preferential rents for apartments where several families live,
  for housing with substandard sanitary or technical conditions, for
  hostels, for families with income below 80 rubles per member or those
  whose living conditions are below the accepted social norm;
- to annul the normative acts that give certain categories of people the
  right to additional floor space, as well as preferential rents for the
  personnel of state organizations and enterprises, professional, Party,
  and other public organizations, military commanders, and members of
  the bar and medical workers practicing at home;
- to draft and introduce in 1990 regulations on the lease of housing from
  nongovernmental stock, which provide for the establishment of contract rents, with local soviets having the right to establish a ceiling for
  such rents.

The rise in rent and lease payment must proceed concurrently with the
indexation of incomes, including revision of the subsistence minimum and
indexation of pensions, allowances, and scholarships.

We must solve the problem of the state's debts, that is, the problem of
those who have been waiting to have their living conditions improved, as
well as change the principles and forms of the free provision of housing.
With this aim in view local soviets can take the following measures:

- everyone on the waiting list will have the right either to continue
  waiting or to quit, in the latter case receiving compensation, in propor-

tion to the time spent waiting for an apartment, from the local soviet for buying an apartment on the free housing market;

- changing the system of free provision of housing through the use of cheap municipal housing allotted on the basis of strict norms;
- republics may independently change the criteria for registering those who want to improve their living standards, depending on the per capita income or the floor space which that person or persons have, or both;
- priority in the distribution of municipal housing will be given to the socially least protected categories (pensioners, invalids, and sick persons).

The people on the housing waiting lists can be regarded as people paying fees for the apartment they would receive sometime in the future (with every year worth one-thirtieth or one-twenty-fifth of the cost of an apartment). The number of years spent waiting for an apartment will determine the compensation, which will not be paid out in cash by the soviet, but will be deducted from the purchase price when the person in question receives an apartment.

It would be expedient to establish specialized housing banks or funds for the issue of such credits, the resources for which could be secured by the sale of new housing, including blocks of apartments, at market prices, in cash and later on credit. Profits from these operations could be used to extend credits to those waiting for an apartment, as well as to build and buy cheap municipal housing.

The purchase of all-new housing is an important principle of housing reform. Taking into account the social complications that would accompany this reform in this country, we suggest that this principle be applied gradually.

Already in 1991 some new apartments and blocks of apartments could be sold at their full cost. We must establish a system for crediting the purchase of housing - specifically from local soviets. As a rule, credit will be extended through small down payments and at low interest. Calculations show that the sale of one million apartments (one-third of the current new housing stock) could earn the state 32-33 billion rubles in current prices. Thus, the sale of some 100,000 state-built apartments in 1991 could earn the state some 3 billion rubles.

In 1991 we will start the transfer of departmental housing, together with the maintenance services and their material plant, to local soviets.

A part of this housing stock will be turned over or sold to housing associations and cooperatives, as well as specialized commercial companies.

The successful development of the housing market is possible only through a dramatic increase in housing construction. To achieve this aim we must elaborate specialized republican and national programs that will create conditions for:

- the large-scale redistribution of investments in housing construction and repairs of the existing housing stock through a radical reduction in the construction of industrial facilities and in the investment demand of material production industries, and the transfer of released building capacity to the construction of housing; and
- the demonopolization of the construction business and the restructuring of the economic mechanism of construction, including transformation of the state construction organizations into joint-stock companies, and the lease and establishment of construction cooperatives and noncommercial construction companies under local soviets.

7

The Nonmarket Sector

During the transition to a market economy it is essential to support and consolidate the nonmarket sector, that is, those sectors and types of activity whose value cannot be measured by commercial criteria but whose existence and results are vitally important for society. The nonmarket sector holds a place of prominence in the economy of any developed country, and its condition largely characterizes the country's development level and degree of civilization. The nonmarket sector includes fundamental science, a greater part of the health services and education, culture and art, environmental protection, etc.

The market and nonmarket sectors are linked in the following way: relying on economic incentives, the market sector, which embraces the production of goods and services, augments public wealth. The greater the public wealth, the greater the share of it that can be allocated for the development of the nonmarket sector. This also influences not only the social and moral aspects of the life of society but also production. However, this influence is of a long-term and indirect nature and cannot be measured by traditional yardsticks or estimated in terms of money.

In the long run, an underdeveloped nonmarket sector will adversely affect the entire economy.

Presently, the problem is that during the transition to a market economy, a rigid financial policy may endanger the branches of the nonmarket sector, the condition of which is critical as it is. In this context, we need a clear and coherent policy in this matter.

It will be based on the following principles:

1. Undiminished state support for the branches of the nonmarket sector. The funds to finance them are allocated with due regard to a possible

price increase (indexation of budget allocations) or in constant shares of the sum of budget revenues;

2. The utmost mobilization of public resources for the maintenance and development of the institutions of the nonmarket sector;

3. Commercialization of part of the activities of these branches, which thereby could be transferred to the market sector without any damage to society; clear-cut legislative delimitation of the status of commercial and noncommercial organizations;

4. Organizational and economic restructuring of the activity of the institutions of the non-market sector with a view to ensuring the most effective use of the resources allocated to them.

In the sphere of **health care**, it is envisaged to strive to make medical treatment and disease prevention service consistently accessible to all, to develop a network of free state medical establishments to satisfy the needs of the population which cannot otherwise be met.

With regard to other medical services, the population should have an opportunity to choose noncommercial or commercial medical establishments that will provide paid services of a higher quality, engage in all kinds of "medicine for the healthy" and attend those who need care, not medical treatment.

The development of social services which would attend to the disabled and aged is a priority task for the health services, local authorities, and the public at large.

The state will finance the health services by making direct allocations to the maintenance of medical establishments and by paying the patients' bills according to fixed prices. This will make it possible for them to choose the establishment whose services, paid or free, they would prefer to use, taking into account the degree of expenses to be reimbursed.

Medical insurance should become important. It presupposes covering expenses on medical treatment, disease prevention, and care of patients from special insurance funds provided from budget allocations and contributions made by enterprises and individual citizens. Insurance funds can act as an influential defender of workers' rights in cases where the damage to a worker's health was someone's fault (jobs with conditions hazardous to health, inadequate labor safety) by recovering rehabilitation costs from the responsible parties. There will also be health-care inspectors to audit the quality and expense of health services.

In the field of **science**, the state finances fundamental research and, together with interested partners, promising research projects capable of making breakthroughs in crucial economic sectors.

It is important that the state should change its attitude to science, which should be freed from all forms of bureaucratic management. The Academy of Sciences of the USSR and of the Union republics and sectoral academies will be relieved of administrative functions and turned into public organizations run by the scientific community on democratic principles in conditions of complete openness, with public discussion of proposals and projects which require financing, denying a monopoly to individual scientific schools.

Institutes and other research establishments shall be withdrawn from the academies' jurisdiction. Full independence will be given to universities and colleges, with the management of them by the State Committee for Public Education abolished.

In the aggregate, they will form free organizations combining research and the training of highly skilled personnel and capable of attracting the whole of the nation's intellectual potential.

The bulk of applied research and projects is done on a commercial basis or financed by enterprises. The research and technology market will be formed, R & D institutes will be restructured and expanded with the aim of encouraging initiative and competition by removing the monopolies of the leading institutes. The creation of small research and engineering firms, financed from innovation and risk funds, will be encouraged.

In the field of **education**, the state will finance secondary and special secondary schools, vocational schools, refresher courses, and higher educational establishments. However, the work of the latter is to be restructured so as to make both the teaching staff and the students interested in drastically raising the quality of instruction. Local authorities will have an opportunity to levy taxes for education needs. Enterprises should be encouraged to invest in education.

Decentralization and democratization of management and the encouragement of work on a voluntary basis have to play an important role in the development of education at all levels. Educational establishments will be more independent in shaping their curricula, selecting personnel, and regulating the composition of the student body.

Questions regarding which control bodies should be established locally, their functions and staff, the borders and composition of school districts, the establishment of educational centers, and the distribution of funds for education should be decided by local soviets with the participation of the public.

The most important task regarding improvement of the educational system is the creation of favorable conditions for displaying initiative, freedom of realization of the creative potential for people possessing the methods and art of teaching, and opening of opportunities for competition in a given sphere.

In order to accomplish this task it is necessary to expand in parallel to the free state institutions, a network of private educational institutions charging tuition, which provide possibilities for education and professional training at an especially high-quality level.

Also, it is possible to have noncommercial educational institutions independent from the state and financed by enterprises, and public funding for fulfillment of research projects and developments.

At the same time, world experience shows that the main burden of expenses for education should be undertaken by the state. However, for achieving high standards of education and professional training and for concentrating efforts and means for those purposes, union programs and centers financed from the union budget are required. According to the estimates of specialists, the share of the union budget in total state expenditure for education should amount to 8 to 10 percent.

With the aim of strengthening the interest of the students in higher education for professional training and improving their material well-being, the practice of granting long-term loans for education with subsequent repayment should be expanded alongside the payment of scholarships.

At the same time, the proposed measures in the sphere of education will not be carried out according to the principle "all of them at once and everywhere." The efficacy and depth of the transformations and the rapidity of their implementation in each link should be combined with discretion and gradualism in the choice and preparation of each project. In this sphere also, emphasis is placed not on a unified program and action on command, but on the initiative and enterprise of a large number of people, on removing any regulations which restrict them.

In the sphere of **culture and art** a policy will be set for support, preservation, and restoration of cultural and historical heritage, of aesthetic experience, and creative research and the development of the cultural initiatives of the population. The development of market relations results in certain risks connected with the pursuit of commercial success to the detriment of activities which are socially more valuable but do not find wide demand. With an imperfect market, insufficient financing of culture by the state, and the underdevelopment of patronage, acute problems arise in satisfying the public interest with a low quality and narrow range of cultural activities.

Therefore, in a situation of rapid transition to a market economy, the role of economic support on the part of the society and the state of socially important activities in the sphere of culture and art becomes extremely important.

As priority measures it is necessary to:

1. Elaborate and adopt programs of urgent measures for preservation of national cultures, cultural centers, projects and organizations of national importance; ensure the work of libraries and museums at a distinguished level and allot additional resources for those purposes. The budget of this sphere becomes the main indicator of the actual attitude of society and the legal authorities toward preservation of culture.

2. Encourage allocations for culture from nonbudget sources. It is necessary to offer preferences for patrons: the enterprises, cooperatives, organizations, and citizens transferring funds for development in the social and cultural sphere. It is necessary to have a public atmosphere, a system of material incentives favorable for patronage. Establishment of temporary financial funds for supporting cultural activity should be encouraged by all means.

Simultaneously, serious organizational and economic transformations in the sphere of culture are also required. The system of state financing for the development of culture needs to be restructured. The idea is to renounce the practice of financing state cultural establishments irrespective of the direction and character of their activity and its correspondence to actual requirements. The facilities allotted by the state for the development of culture should be concentrated in project oriented centralized and regional funds and should be allotted for implementation of specific programs and projects on a tender basis.

Cultural-development funds should be formed as state and public funds. The budget remains an important source of their endowment. Decision-making for concrete expenditures should be entrusted to the fund councils, comprised of cultural figures and representatives of the public. When establishing special purpose funds it is necessary to ensure, to a certain extent, their duplication and transfer in order to lessen the bias of the decisions adopted.

In the sphere of culture, just as in the whole social and cultural complex, there may coexist organizations which differ in principle by their status and economic conditions, i.e., commercial (cost-accounting) and noncommercial ones. Commercial organizations will work under market conditions and will obtain the means, including possible budget allocations, in exchange for concrete work results, noncommercial ones for certain parameters of the process of the activity proper. A possible excess of these means over expenses cannot serve as a source for increasing pay for the employees and profit of their owners. Public principles in the management of noncommercial organizations should be represented, first of all, by the bodies of the type of trustee councils. Such a model will allow, provided the labor is paid befittingly, for the implementation of many socially valuable kinds of activity. For its introduction, however, it is necessary to have a special law on non-commercial organizations.

In the sphere of **environmental control and ecological safety,** our country faces especially difficult and urgent tasks. In the process of long-term development, this country lost one of its major components - maintenance of the natural and ecological balance of the people's economy.

As a result, the health of the population was undermined. Already now almost every fourth citizen of the USSR is chronically ill, including at least every sixth child. Ecological strains caused by the grave condition of the environment (in residence, work, and recreation areas) and low ecological quality of the microstructure of vital functions of the population (foodstuffs, drinking water, housing, technology, etc.) devalue the efforts aimed at increasing people's welfare and social reorientation of the economy.

Environmental restriction on the location of production facilities has become a major obstacle to the growth of the range and effectiveness of the economy. This becomes apparent primarily in the shutdown of harmful production facilities and the prohibition on commissioning new ones and modernizing existing enterprises in industrial centers. The standards of ecological damage have been exceeded in most industrial centers. Such prohibitions force the development of additional facilities in new areas which have no infrastructure but have unstable natural systems and higher specific expenses for all kinds of works.

The nonregulated process of withdrawal of ecologically dangerous enterprises causes a chain reaction of imbalance in the economy. The potential scale of this problem in our country is determined by violation of ecological norms practically everywhere. In 1989 due to ecological reasons work was stopped at over 1000 large enterprises and production units. At the same time, purely administrative counteraction to these processes only intensifies the confrontation between the center, enterprises, local government bodies, and the population and strengthens the political emphasis of the ecological movement.

The number of large-scale accidents at production facilities with the most hazardous emissive pollution of contaminants increases. Illustrative of the scale of possible economic damage are the expenses for mitigating the aftereffects of the Chernobyl accident, which will reach 25 billion rubles by 1991. The modern scale of ecological disasters, and the need to compensate for losses as a result of natural calamities (the gravity of which is to a considerable degree due to insufficient regard for ecological and natural restrictions) create a real threat of switching the released resources of the economy from solving the strategic tasks of forming the new structure of the economy to maintaining its present potential. The stabilization of the situation in the Aral and Caspian areas alone requires, according to the available estimate, 16.5 billion rubles of capital investments in the next five years.

The above-mentioned adverse natural and ecological trends must be overcome under any changes of the social and economic course.

A key to forming long-term natural and ecological policy is the realization of the gravity of the present situation as a result of the accumulation, for many decades, of structural deformations of the economy: the domination of nature-intensive industries, the extremely heavy costs of obsolete nature-intensive technologies, the raw-material export orientation, the absence of human values among the real priorities of social and economic policy, and the destruction of the culture of labor and consumption.

Radical improvement of the ecological situation in the country can be achieved only as a result of successful implementation of the proposed economic reform for the economy's restructuring and only by moving forward in solving other major social and economic tasks. It will require major renovation of production facilities, improvement of foreign economic relations, and transformation of direct expenses for ecological needs into a major component of the load on the economy. Direct capital investments in environmental control and rationalization of nature management necessary for achieving minimum modern standards by 2005-2010 are estimated at 260 - 340 billion rubles, i.e., they are comparable with the expenses for other major special-purpose programs.

In view of the limitation of available resources, in parallel with strategic goals, natural and ecological policy in the coming years will be determined by the necessity of solving the most acute problems which today block the resolution of other urgent social tasks.

The high resource-intensity of radical solutions for natural and ecological problems, unpreparedness for full-scale deployment of large programs, and toughening of economic restrictions, in combination with the real possibility of the ecological obstruction of a number of the most important directions of economic development, require an apportionment of a special natural and ecological package of urgent measures for the nearest transitional period.

The peculiarity of this package is the limitation of the range of tasks which it embraces to two major ones: maintenance of the minimum level of ecological safety and creation of stocks for a consecutive transition to implementing major natural and ecological programs.

The first direction includes the implementation of special-purpose programs pooling the efforts of the center and the republics for normalization of the situation in the national zones of ecological disaster. The composition, status, financing terms, and conditions and provision of resources by these zones should be legislatively approved by the end of 1990.

It will be necessary to urgently elaborate and implement a complex of measures aimed at radically increasing ecological safety and accident-free operation of economic projects. The priority of this task is determined by high probability of an increased rate of accidents, first of all in connection with the expected aging of capital goods and secondly as a result of the intensification of production irregularities.

At present compensation for damage caused by others and for natural calamities is borne by the state, which results in the practically complete economic irresponsibility of the direct culprits. This can be eliminated by introduction of mandatory accident and insurance funds for enterprises. Their size should be determined by the results of special inventories evaluating the real damage — taking into account the actual state of major production funds — and not the supposed ecological danger of accidents of various classes, as well as natural calamities and a respective evaluation of the expenses required for compensation of potential damage. Periodically taking such inventories for the reevaluation of the accident and insurance funds of the enterprises will stimulate them to reduce the level of accident danger, allowing the return of money from those funds to working capital.

Similar regional and republican funds should be established by applying premiums from the accident and insurance funds of the enterprises, as well as the state, republican, and local budgets. The main directions of expenditure of their money are: the compensation of damages and the execution of restoration work at a scale inaccessible to enterprises, the organization and maintenance of antiaccident services and reserves, communications systems, carrying out of special-purpose research and development works, and financing of measures increasing ecological safety.

It is necessary to adopt additional measures for maintaining an actual minimum scale for direct environmental activities, preserving at least a technical, organizational, and economic potential in this sphere. In 1989, as compared with average indicators for 1986-1988, treatment amounted to 16 percent of capacity for all water supply facilities, 34 percent for circulated water, and for air pollution abatement — 38 percent. One solution is an increase of coverage of environmental-protection measures by state orders and tax privileges. The same privileges should be expanded to cover the products and services which are directly used for fulfillment of environmental-protection measures. These measures seem to be more effective than a return to the fixing of norms of financing allotted for ecological needs and restriction of consumption of natural resources which have become widespread at present.

The stalled process of reorganization of governmental bodies for control and management of the state of natural resources and the environment should be expedited.

Effective approaches to the problems of the most ecology-intensive production facilities and the acute social conflicts that arise around them can be found only on the basis of forming violence-free compromise mechanisms as their solution. An urgent measure here is the setting up of an agreement with the parties concerned and the local soviets over the periods of time for withdrawal of the most dangerous projects, their reconstruction, or the additional equipping of treatment facilities (to be determined in view of the actual time required for creating compensating employment, commissioning new facilities, etc.), elaboration of the required guarantees for fulfillment of agreements, and their confirmation by authorized government bodies.

The same goal is pursued by the introduction of direct ecological privileges to the population residing in unfavorable areas, as well as in the territories with proposed commissioning of large ecology-intensive projects (including priority provision for unleaded gasoline, other "pure" products, advantages in the supply of products based on ecology-intensive production facilities, etc.) in exchange for immediate liquidation of "dirty" production facilities.

Regarding the evidently prolonged conflicts inevitable in the near future concerning the most ecology-intensive and ecology-hazardous projects, special laws should be adopted determining the form of their settlement (similar to the legal norms of strike regulations).

Measures in the second direction are aimed at increasing the purposeful implementation of the most effective solutions, establishment of a material base for production of the necessary volume of high quality treatment equipment and instrumentation, and formation of the economic and organizational mechanisms of a regulated market economy.

The primary condition for solving all of the above-mentioned tasks is the expeditious development of a network of control over the state of the environment. In this sphere one of the key measures is handing over to the USSR State Committee for Environment Control the means and functions of the general customer in the design and production of the respective instrumentation base at the enterprises of the defense industry, which will undergo a change in their range of manufactured products. It will be necessary to sharply expand the manufacture of the simplest individual means of ecological control, and its range and distribution channels should be determined with active participation of the nature-protection movement.

To guarantee the required high growth in production of treatment equipment and instrumentation, and the improvement of its quality, it will be necessary to form a special ecological dominion in the defense industry; this conversion should be made a top priority at the legislative level. This dominion has good prospects for defense enterprises as well because it will allow them to preserve a research-intensive orientation and to avoid sharp falloffs in the standards of supply efficiency, labor productivity, etc.

Under market conditions, a most important role should be played by the setting of quotas by local soviets for environmental pollution (at minimum, realistically achievable levels of discharge for operating enterprises), payment for these discharge quotas and initially small (taking into account the financial possibilities of enterprises) but sharply growing fines (which will grow dramatically in view of the actual damage, at the beginning of approved period for withdrawal of ecologically-intensive projects), for discharges above the norms at the rate of the full amount of the profits obtained by violating the quotas. The practice, adopted abroad by regional authorities ,of selling the "rights to pollute," with subsequent payable rotation among the enterprises of the region, should also be tried.

On the basis of the above-mentioned payments and fines, a multilevel system of ecological funds should be formed with strict, special-purpose utilization of funds and with projects chosen by the highest bid.

With the aim of radically improving nature management, urgent measures are necessary for the preparation and introduction of payment (tax) for the use of natural resources, the land, and irrecoverable natural resources, and an increase of payment, up to an economically justified level, for water and forest use. Work on the evaluation of resources should be expedited, and in 1990, practical proposals should already be prepared for restructuring of economic relations in the organization of management in this sphere.

A legally fixed share of the tax for the use of nonrenewable natural resources should be directed into the local budgets. Thus, it will stimulate their activity in evaluating natural resources and creating organizational mechanisms for the calculation and collection of taxes.

Prohibition on the commissioning of new or expanded operating facilities in those areas with an unfavorable ecological situation should be replaced by a new, fixed-by-law mandatory inclusion into the programs of the construction of new enterprises and reconstruction of existing enterprises of special packages of ecological measures, ensuring a reduction of total pollution of the environment within the region.

Declarations should be urgently introduced to maximize ecological and ergometric parameters for products and projects (including imported ones), and rigid economic sanctions should be envisaged for exceeding the announced standards in practice.

As a whole, the direct capital investments for 1991-1995 can be estimated within a range of from 15 billion rubles (which actually means the maintenance of their accumulated effects and has at least the minimum material and technical provisions) up to 45-48 billion rubles. The authenticity of the latest estimates, which are based on the urgency of radical improvement of the natural and ecological situation, depends on a revision of the conversion program (bringing the average annual volume of production of equipment and materials for ecological purposes with capacity for a modified range of products to 2 billion rubles), as well as on the recognition by the public of the feasibility of moving forward in the ecological sphere in an essentially expeditious manner, as compared with other priority directions in social and economic development.

PART IV

LEGISLATIVE AND ORGANIZATIONAL SUPPORT FOR ECONOMIC REFORM

Legislative and Organizational Support for Economic Reform

Successful implementation of economic reform is possible only with harmonized actions of all the republics, such as elaboration of common principles, scenarios, and the timing of transformations. Besides, the legislative basis of the economic reform and the organizational mechanisms of its implementation are to be devised within the shortest time. A part of the necessary laws and standard acts have already been adopted by the Supreme Councils of the USSR and the Union republics. However, these laws were not mutually coordinated and what really matters is that the minimum array of the legislative acts required for accelerated implementation of the reform is not workable.

The package of necessary laws and standard acts is to be worked out together with the Reform Program and should be enacted simultaneously on the whole territory of the USSR. It can be done by promulgating ordinances of the Union President. The republics can either ratify these laws, pass their own with amendments, or introduce changes to the laws already in force. The main condition is to observe the fundamental principles fixed when signing the Economic Union of sovereign states.

The following fundamental laws are proposed for adoption:

The first group - on monetary and financial regulation of the economy:

- on the Reserve System of the Union as the union of the central banks of the republics;
- on the single monetary system;
- on banks and banking;
- on the budget structure;
- on the public debt.

The second group—on entrepreneurship, competition, and privatization of property:

- on free entrepreneurship;
- on land-tenure reform;
- on the Fund of State Property of the USSR;
- on the circulation of securities and securities exchanges;
- on the restriction of monopolistic activities and promotion of competition.

The third group - on foreign economic relations:

- on foreign trade and its regulation;
- on foreign investments and their protection;
- on exchange control and regulation;
- on the customs system.

The fourth group - on social protection of the population:

- on employment;
- on income indexation for the population.

Simultaneously, with adoption of new laws, the force of legislative acts which conflict with the new laws will be repealed (suspended).

ORGANIZATIONAL SUPPORT
FOR ECONOMIC REFORM

A program of transformation approved by the Supreme Soviet of the USSR and the parliaments of the republics should be used as a basis for implementing the economic reforms. The economic reform concept should be coordinated and adopted as early as September-October 1990.

The Economic Reform Program itself consists of the following blocks:

- the concept of the program;
- well-developed detailed programs for the various directions of transformation;
- packages of draft laws;
- standards and procedures documents arranged in various guidelines;
- flow charts of the program with the appropriate blocks arranged in a time-ordered sequence, to ensure the possibility of alternative actions;
- estimates.

In conjunction with the detailed explanations of individual positions on economic reform, it is necessary to take complete stock of state property, exchange and financial assets. Only in this case will the program be realistic and unexpected failures avoided.

In the course of the preparatory period, it is advisable not to adopt any new decisions which change the economic situation if they are not in any way linked with the general direction and concept of the reform (specifically, decisions about supplementary social programs, new foreign loans, liquidation of the bank debts of some enterprises, and introduction of money substitutes).

At the same time some measures of the economic reform which do not require long preparation should be launched without delay.

REORGANIZATION OF MANAGEMENT STRUCTURES

For the period of reform, the executive authorities which implement the reform will be accorded exclusive rights within their domain of responsibility. There will be a clear-cut delimitation of powers between the legislative and executive authority and between levels of economic management (local soviets of the republic - the Union).

The following structures of executive bodies which directly implement the economic reform are recommended for the sovereign republics and local soviets:

- a commission on reform or a reform division at a single Ministry of Economy;
- a committee on state property management which is directly involved in the privatization of property;
- an anti-monopoly committee;
- a committee on land-tenure reform;
- a committee on support of small business and new economic structures;
- a committee on employment and public works.

The newly established organizational structure is the Reform Program, which was completed utilizing the specifics of the socioeconomic situation of the republic, the standards and procedures documentation, and the new economic laws. The employees of these state bodies should take refresher courses and have direct access to statistics.

Simultaneously with the onset of the transformation and according to the Agreement on the Economic Union, governing bodies are to be reorganized. They are to be set up on a basis of equal representation of the republics-sovereign states, and the corresponding powers, which are delegated by the republics to the Union bodies and envisaged by the agreement. Sectorial ministries and the Bureau of the Council of Ministers of the USSR on production complexes are to be dissolved. The functions of the bodies managing those spheres of activity which demand single management on a Union scale should be clearly defined. Professional skills are the main criteria for selection of personnel for the reorganized structures.

The Union economy's governing bodies can be established under the guidance of the President of the USSR. For the period of economic transformation and stabilization, an interrepublican economic committee with very wide powers will be set up.

INFORMATION SUPPORT

Senseless secrecy in the sphere of economic statistics hinders the process of reform. A scientific analysis of the country's socioeconomic situation and proper international comparisons are impossible when there is a desire for monopolizing the truth and embellishing reality.

Management of the transformation process and timely responses to new developments call for serious changes in the system of collecting and processing statistics:

1. Provide openness and accessibility of economic information;
2. Withdraw the State Committee of the USSR for Statistics and the entire system of statistics institutions from the jurisdiction of the Council of Ministers of the USSR and other executive bodies;
3. Publish economic statistics using the methodology accepted worldwide, both in centralized practice (by the State Committee of the USSR for Statistics) and by ministries, departments, authorities in the form of collections of documents, journals, and statistical yearbooks;
4. Outline the range of data to be published regularly in the central press;
5. Publish, at regular intervals, the methodology for estimating statistics;

THE ORGANIZATIONAL STRUCTURE OF
ECONOMIC REFORM MANAGEMENT

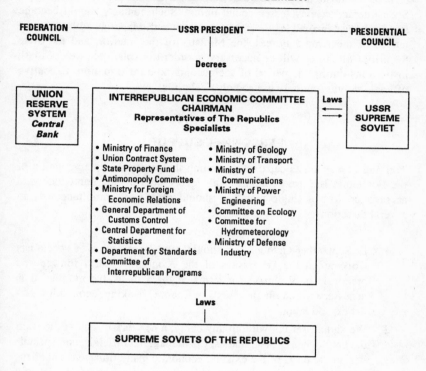

6. Define, legally, the right of statistical organizations to receive primary economic information;

7. Establish, in statistical organizations, socioeconomic monitoring systems, the task of which will be to follow up, regulate, and forecast economic processes.

When economic transformation begins, feedback mechanisms between the governing bodies and the population will be of special importance.

Openness in the preliminary arrangements for reform and its implementation, including intensive **elucidative** work in the mass media, is a must.

Top-level state officials who implement reform should have constant contacts with mainstream political movements, parties, and professional groups. Such interaction may lessen social unrest. Such contacts should become standard practice at all levels of state management. Meetings with representatives of the Armed Forces, the Ministry of the Interior, and the State Security Committee will be necessary in order to explain the role of these institutions during the period of socioeconomic transformation. Executive officials should routinely use sociological polls.

PERSONNEL SUPPORT

Training of specialists capable of running the practical implementation of the Economic Reform Program at all levels should start immediately in accordance with a single plan and should spread out simultaneously in several directions:

1. In September-October, we should send large teams of specialists working on the key issues of the economic reform for focused practical study abroad for terms of three to twelve months. It is necessary to retrain specialists in finance, banking, economics, statistics, and labor.

2. We should set up, without any delay, a network of courses to train the employees of state bodies, top managerial officials, and specialists on the basis of the existing economic institutions and establishments. Retraining syllabi are to be drawn up on the basis of newly prepared standards and procedures documents. The training cycle should last 20 to 30 days, and up-to-date training methods should be used. The employees of academic institutes, joint ventures, educational establishments, and Soviet foreign offices and establishments should be invited to become teachers and instructors of such courses.

3. We should address governments and firms in Western countries and request that they host Soviet students, postgraduates, and young specialists for economic and commercial training for up to five-year terms.

4. We should invite foreign specialists to establish elements of a market infrastructure (commodity and securities exchanges, investment funds, and job-finding systems), and also to elaborate and implement certain directions of reform.

5. Introduce, without any delay, in all economic higher educational establishments of the country, courses on general economic theory, market economy, and the study of diversified models of its operation. Ensure the rapid translation of Western standard economic textbooks.

PART V

SUPPLEMENT

SUPPLEMENT

ON THE INFORMATION NOT RECEIVED
BY THE WORKING GROUP FROM
THE MINISTRIES AND DEPARTMENTS

In order to analyze the availability of potential economic reserves and account for them as part of the reform to stabilize the standard of living and compensate for the rupture of economic ties, the government ministries of the USSR and the RSFSR were requested to provide appropriate information. Requests for that information were sent to 21 addresses and signed by Stanislaw Shatalin, a member of the Presidential Council.

The information assisted the working group considerably. Some ministries and departments of the USSR failed to provide the requested information — information which in some cases concerned crucial aspects of current economic conditions. This created considerable problems and made it impossible to carry out many important calculations. Listed below is the information that was requested but not made available by August 31, 1990.

1. USSR Gosplan (Government Planning Agency)

The Planning Agency failed to make available the following information:

1. The aggregate financial balance of the state for the years 1980 and 1985 through 1990;

2. The intersectoral balances for 1985, 1987, and 1988. Information about the Defense Ministry was requested, but none was made available;

3. Balances for the cash income and spending of the population planned and reported for the years 1980 and 1985 through 1990 for the RSFSR and the USSR;

4. Aggregate balances for capital investment planned and reported for 1980 and 1985 through 1990;

5. The results of the inventory of uncompleted construction projects for 1990;

6. The amount and structure of investments exceeding limits (planned and actual) for 1985 through 1990.

The USSR State Planning Committee (GOSPLAN) completely ignored the working group's request for information. It made available only outdated computations of its Main Computing Center, which proved to be of no practical value for the working group.

2. USSR Finance Ministry

The Finance Ministry failed to make available the following information:

1. The breakdown of the USSR state budget concerning the system of budgets for 1980, 1985-1988, and quarterly figures for 1989-1990. The information sent to the working group about the USSR state budget is not reliable and not significantly different from published reports.

2. The aggregate foreign currency plan (balance of payments of the USSR) covering the types of currency for 1970, 1980, 1985-1988, and 1989-1990 (quarterly breakdown). The absence of that information made it impossible to comprehensively analyze the currency situation of the USSR and to account for it in the reform program.

3. The gold and precious metal reserves of the USSR in tons and millions of dollars for 1970 and 1980-1989.

4. The aggregate financial balance of the state for 1980 and 1985-1990.

The absence of these crucial data in the report sent by the USSR Finance Ministry shows that for all intents and purposes it ignored the request of the working group. The ministry made available data of secondary importance.

3. USSR Vnesheconombank

The bank totally ignored the group's request for information and failed to make available the following crucial data:

I. Finances

1. The size and structure of the USSR's foreign debt and the debts owed to the USSR for 1970, 1980, 1985-1990 (countries, types and deadlines of credits, including hard-currency credits), and the structure of spending on foreign-debt servicing.

2. The size and structure of Soviet deposits abroad (hard-currency reserves) for 1980-1989 and 1990 (quarterly) by durations and countries.

3. An analytical memorandum on the duration and size of debt repayment by other countries and the possibility for debt sales on the international currency market and deadlines and amounts of repayment, and the costs of servicing the USSR's external debt for 1990, 1991, 1992, 1993, 1994, 1995, 1996-2000.

4. The overall balance of Soviet banks abroad for 1980 and 1985-1990.

II. Credit

1. Credit plans and progress reports for 1980 and 1985-1989, and cash-turnover statistics and analyses for 1990 (quarterly).

4.The State Foreign Economic Commission of the USSR Council of Ministers

Part of the requested information was made available. However, the commission failed to provide certain crucial data:

1. The size and structure of the USSR's external debt for 1970, 1980, and 1985-1990 (countries, deadlines, types of credits, including hard-currency credits), and the structure of spending on foreign debt servicing.

2. The size and structure of Soviet deposits abroad (hard-currency reserves) for 1980-1989 and 1990 (quarterly), duration and countries.

3. An analytical memorandum on the deadlines and sums of debt repayment by other countries, the possibility of selling debts on the world credit market, etc., as well as the deadlines and size of repayment and the costs of servicing the external debt of the USSR for 1990, 1991, 1992, 1993, 1994, 1995, 1996-2000.
4. The overall balance of Soviet banks abroad for 1980 and 1985-1990.

5. USSR Defense Ministry

The USSR Defense Ministry did not make available the information requested.

6.

No information was made available by the managerial offices of the Central Committees of the:
CPSU
YCL,
The All-Union Central Council of Trade Unions

7. The USSR State Committee for Prices (Goskomtsen)

Goskomtsen failed to make available the requested information. However, it sent an analytical memorandum of some interest (though not the information requested by the group).

The following institutions fully complied with the request for information on time:

- USSR Promstrobank
- USSR Sberbank
- USSR Gosbank
- USSR Agroprombank
- USSR Zhilsotsbank
- USSR Goskomstat
- USSR Gossnab
- USSR Foreign Ministry
- USSR Council of Ministers' State Commission for Food and Procurement

Other ministries and government departments of the USSR and RSFSR provided incomplete or irrelevant information and did not meet the deadline.

THE CONSUMER MARKET

The situation in the consumer market is critical. It is determined to a great extent by the dynamics of farm production. The rate of production on the farms resembles a decaying curve tending toward zero growth (Figure 1) despite the growing investment in the agroindustrial complex. The growth of retail trade turnover in the eighties was highly unstable. It was influenced by changes in the import policy of the state, which opposed the economic trends appearing in the country and tended to increase fluctuations instead of smoothing them over (Figure 3). The disintegration of the consumer market was "programmed" in 1986 and 1987 when no action was taken to increase consumer goods imports or stimulate consumer goods production in the country.

The dramatic increase in the growth rate of retail trade turnover in 1989 and 1990 (up to 10 to 12 percent) and a 19 percent increase in import purchases was late by one or two years. The natural consequence of this was the accelerating imbalance between the incomes and expenditures of the population and growing shortages in the consumer market (Figures 4 and 5). The money in circulation kept on growing but the greater part of its growth was surplus and could not be spent.

According to VNIIKS data the availability of staple foodstuffs declined from 90 percent in 1983 to 22 percent in 1989 and 11 percent in the middle of 1990. A similar situation emerged with respect to consumer goods, household goods, and durables.

As a result the prices charged by the collective farm market for staple foodstuffs exceeded those charged by state stores in the 1980's by 100 to 150 percent.

One cannot avoid remarking that the government program unveiled in May had a destructive effect on the consumer market. The announced intention to raise prices by at least 100 percent signaled the end of public confidence. As a result, food prices on the collective-farm market and the prices of consumer goods on the black market experienced a runaway growth. The national savings bank (Sberbank) reported zero growth in deposits (forecast: 5-6 billion rubles), i.e., that money remained in the hands of the population, resulting in the "fulfillment of the annual plan" for increasing the cash money supply by the middle of the year.

FIGURES

Fig. 1
RATE OF GROWTH OF PRODUCTION ON THE FARMS

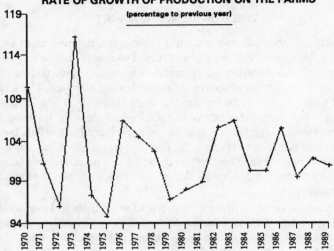

(percentage to previous year)

Fig. 2
RATE OF GROWTH OF PRODUCTION IN CONSUMER GOODS INDUSTRIES

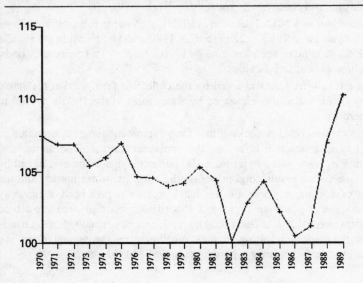

Fig. 3
**RATIO BETWEEN RETAIL TRADE TURNOVER GROWTH AND CONSUMER
GOODS INDUSTRIES PRODUCTION GROWTH RATE**

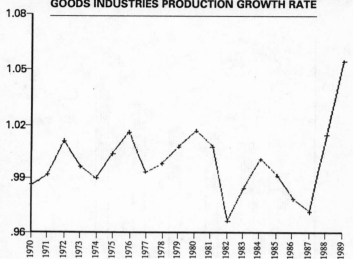

Fig. 4
**RATIO BETWEEN SPENDING BY POPULATION
(WITHOUT SAVINGS) TO INCOME**

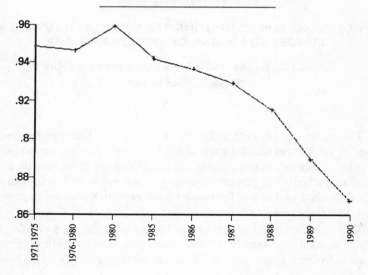

Fig. 5
CASH IN CIRCULATION
(billions of rubles)

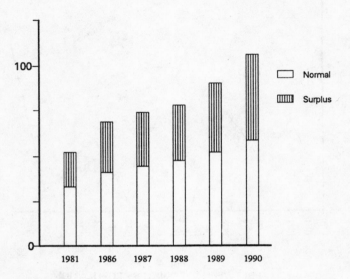

PROCEDURE FOR COMPUTING THE MINIMUM CONSUMER
BUDGET FOR A MAN OF EMPLOYABLE AGE

Drawn Up by the USSR State Committee for Labor
(Goskomtrud) in 1989

The minimum consumer budget describes a consumption pattern and a level of satisfaction which society at a given time considers the minimum possible. It is a calculated quantity and is significantly dependent on computation methods. The procedures employed at present are tied in with the actual standard of living of the poorest families, which is closer to poverty than the low-income bracket.

That approach gears the minimum budget to satisfying physiological requirements at an extremely low level, leaving no room for the development of the individual. That tendency is illustrated very graphically by the proce-

MINIMUM CONSUMER BUDGET FOR A MAN ABLE TO WORK
(in 1988) cost of food.

	Quantity per year	Price (ruble)	Cost per year (ruble)
Wheat flour	9.1	0.31	2.82
Wheat bread	66.7	0.28	18.68
Buns	20.0	0.35	7.00
Vanilla bread	4.3	1.12	4.82
Rye bread	92.0	0.13	11.96
Rice	9.1	0.88	8.01
Millet	9.0	0.28	2.52
Buckwheat	9.0	0.56	5.04
Beans	2.0	0.32	0.64
Macaroni	4.0	0.42	1.68
Vermicelli	3.3	0.38	1.25
Sugar	10.4	0.90	9.36
Refined Sugar	14.4	1.00	14.40
Fruit sweets	5.0	1.30	6.50
Sweets "Vasilyok"	0.2	5.00	1.00
Cream pastries	3.0	0.90	2.70
Biscuits	0.3	1.40	0.42
Strawberry jam	0.5	1.93	0.96
Apple jam	2.0	0.91	1.82
Vegetable oil	10.0	1.65	16.50
Margarine	4.6	1.40	6.44
Beef	20.3	2.00	40.60
Mutton	10.8	1.90	20.52
Pork	10.9	1.90	20.71
Chicken	1.1	2.65	2.91
Geese	1.1	1.80	1.98
Ducks	1.0	1.90	1.90
Sausage for tea	1.1	1.70	1.87
Ukraine sausage	1.1	2.70	2.97
Frankfurters	1.1	1.90	2.09
Cutlets	1.6	1.10	1.76
Preserved meat	2.0	2.57	5.14
Salted pork fat	3.0	2.40	7.20
Grease	2.5	1.60	4.00
Pacific Ocean herring	3.5	0.85	2.97
Far East navaga	2.0	0.80	1.60
Cod	4.0	0.56	2.24
Cod (fillet)	10.0	0.77	7.70
Flat fish	1.0	0.51	0.51
Bream	3.0	0.72	2.16
Sprats in oil	0.3	4.40	1.32
Flat fish in tomato sauce	0.7	1.81	1.27

MINIMUM CONSUMER BUDGET FOR A MAN ABLE TO WORK
(in 1988) cost of food (Continued)

	Quantity per year	Price (ruble)	Cost per year (ruble)
Milk	184.3	0.28	51.60
Sour cream	4.2	1.50	6.30
Condensed milk	—	—	—
Condensed milk without sugar	—	—	—
Curds	11.5	0.85	9.77
Fatless curds	—	0.48	—
Poshekhon cheese	2.0	2.60	5.20
Processed cheese	4.0	1.50	6.00
Butter	3.6	3.50	12.60
Melted butter	—	3.50	—
Eggs	183.0	0.09	16.47
Tea	0.5	7.60	3.80
Other	—	—	1.00
Potatoes	146.0	0.19	27.74
Cabbage	29.8	0.19	5.66
Salted cabbage	15.0	0.16	2.40
Red beets	13.8	0.18	2.48
Carrots	20.2	0.27	5.45
Onions	10.2	0.48	4.90
Tomatoes	18.2	2.13	38.77
Salted tomatoes	3.0	0.30	0.90
Cucumbers	7.4	1.78	13.17
Salted cucumbers	7.4	0.80	5.92
Eggplant paste	1.0	0.72	0.72
Spring onions	3.0	0.50	1.50
Lemons	0.5	3.50	1.75
Oranges	1.0	2.00	2.00
Apples	11.0	0.91	10.01
Pears	2.0	1.10	2.20
Dried plums	3.0	2.00	6.00
Grapes	1.0	1.35	1.35
Conserved fruits	1.8	1.21	2.18
Watermelons	20.0	0.24	4.8

TOTAL:		per year	506.26
		per month	12.19
Expenditure in public catering		per year	101.10
		per month	8.42
Total (including public catering)		per year	607.36
		per month	50.61

STRUCTURE OF MINIMUM CONSUMER BUDGET
FOR AN ABLE-BODIED MAN
In 1988 (the basis for minimum wage)

Expenditure Items	Expenses, in rubles		
	per year	per month	%
Food	612.0	51.0	36.9
Clothes, footwear	409.5	34.12	24.7
Hygiene items and medicines	40.27	3.36	2.4
Furniture and durable goods	227.76	18.98	13.7
Housing and communal services	71.7	5.98	4.3
Culture and recreation	42.3	3.53	2.6
Consumer services	49.03	4.09	3.0
Transport	104.0	8.67	6.3
Communication	36.75	3.06	2.2
Dues	15.0	1.25	0.9
Tobacco	19.8	1.65	1.2
Other items	30.3	2.53	1.8
TOTAL:	**1658.41**	**138.20**	**100.0**

CALCULATION OF EXPENDITURES
FOR COMMUNICATION SERVICES (IN CITY)

	Quantity per year	Exploitation period	Price (ruble)	Cost per year
Installation of a radio	1	10	3.5	0.35
Installation of telephone	1	20	100.0	5.00
Telephone charge		1.0	12.0	
TV antenna charge			0.15	1.8
Letters	10		0.06	0.6
Ordinary telegram 20 words	2		2.0	4.0
Money transfer, 50 ruble	1		1.0	1.0
Payments for intercity Telephone calls				8.0
Parcels 8 kg Distance 500 km	2		2.0	4.0
TOTAL:			per year	36.75
			per month	3.06

CALCULATION OF OTHER EXPENDITURES

Gifts	22.3 rubles per year
Flowers	8.0 rubles per year
TOTAL:	per year—30.3
	per month—2.53

CALCULATION OF EXPENDITURES ON
HYGIENE ITEMS AND MEDICINES

	Amount Needed	Usage Period	Annual Purchase	Price (Ruble)	Cost of Annual Purchases (Ruble)
Bath soap (kg)					
(50 g per wk x 52 wk)					
200 g - 1 piece	2.6	1	2.6	0.19	2.47
Toilet soap (kg)					
(25 g per wk)					
100 g - 1 piece	1.3	1	1.3	0.23	2.99
Soap for other purposes (kg)	1.0	1	1.0	0.23	1.15
Soap for washing clothes (kg)					
1 piece - 200 g	3.0	1	3.0	0.23	3.45
Washing powder (pkg)					
1 package - 1.5 kg	3.0	1	3.0	1.70	5.10
Toothpaste	12	1	12	0.25	3.00
Toothbrush	1	1	1	0.27	0.27
Eau de cologne (bottle)	2	1	2	0.53	1.06
Shaving cream	3	1	3	0.40	1.20
Shoe polish	6	1	6	0.17	1.02
Toilet paper	5	1	5	0.32	0.60
Cotton	2	1	2	0.09	0.18
Bandage	3	1	3	0.10	0.30
Adhesive tape	3	1	3	0.07	0.21
Clyster	1	3	1/3	0.24	0.03
Hot-water bottle	1	1	1/5	0.80	0.16
Thermometer	1	3	1/3	0.42	0.14
Mustard plasters	50	1	50	0.05	0.25
Antiseptic	2	1	2	0.09	0.18
Iodine	2	1	2	0.09	0.18
Valerian	1	1	1	0.12	0.12
Pirkaphen	2	1	2	0.21	0.42
Analgin	2	1	2	0.31	0.62
Vitamins	4	1	4	0.08	0.32
Contraceptives	12	1	12	1.00	12.00
Decongestant nasal spray	1	1	0.40	0.40	
Dish scrubber					1.00
Comb	1	1	1	0.40	0.40
TOTAL	per year				40.27
	per month				3.36

CALCULATION OF EXPENDITURES FOR CULTURAL SERVICES

Kinds of service	Expenditure in rubles
Cinema	12–50
Theater	—
Concerts	4–00
Circus	2–00
Museum and exhibitions	2–00
Parks and discos	5–00
Zoo	—
Excursions	10–00
Stadiums	2–00
Recreation	4–80
Books and periodicals	34–62
TOTAL: per year	76–92
per month	6–41

CALCULATION OF EXPENDITURES FOR CONSUMER SERVICES

Population able to work	49.03 rubles per year
	4.1 rubles per month

LODGING AND COMMUNAL SERVICES

Population able to work	71.7 rubles per year
	5.98 rubles per month

DUES

Population able to work	15 rubles per year
	1.25 ruble per month

CALCULATION OF TRANSPORT EXPENDITURES

			Price (rubles)	Cost per year (rubles)
1.	City transport:			
	a)	trip to work and back 250 working days x 2 = 500	0.10	50.0
	b)	outings to cinema, theater, stadiums, on a visit	0.05	4.0
2.	Intercity transport:			
	a)	excursions to the countryside 20 times x 2 = 40	0.25	10.0
	b)	Holiday round trip (once a year)	20.00	40.0
	TOTAL:		per year	104.0
			per month	8.67

CALCULATION OF EXPENDITURES ON TOBACCO

	Quantity	Price (rubles)	Cost per year (rubles)
Cigarettes (package)	8 x 12 = 96	0.20	19.20
Matches (box)	5 x 12 = 60	0.01	0.80
TOTAL:		per year	20.00
		per month	1.65

CALCULATION OF EXPENDITURES FOR PURCHASING CLOTHES AND FOOTWEAR

		Amount Needed	Usage Period	Annual Purchase	Price in rubles	Cost of Annual Purchase
1.	Winter coat	1	7	1/7	180	25.7
2.	Light overcoat	1	7	1/7	120	17.1
3.	Vest	1	4	1/4	135	33.8
4.	Woolsuit	1	3	1/3	160	53.3
5.	Half-wool suit	1	3	1/3	75	25.0
6.	Raincoat	1	4	1/4	110	27.5
7.	Half-wool trousers	1	2	1/2	27	13.5
8.	Summer trousers	1	2	1/2	24	12.0
9.	Sweaters	2	3	2/3	30	20.0
10.	Shirts	4	2	2	8.50	17.0
11.	Working clothes	1	2	1/2	10	5.0
12.	Pyjamas	1	2	1/2	8	4.0
13.	T-shirt	4	2	2	2.50	5.0
14.	Underwear	2	2	1	8	8.0
15.	Pants	4	2	2	1.40	2.80
16.	Swimming shorts	1	2	1/2	5	2.50
17.	Wool scarf	1	3	1/3	4.50	1.5
18.	Textile scarf	1	3	1/3	3	1.0
19.	Tie	2	3	2/3	2	1.33
20.	Cotton socks	5	1	5	1.00	5.0
21.	Wool socks	1	1	1	2.80	2.8
22.	Fur cap	1	3	1/3	19	6.3
23.	Cap	1	3	1/3	2.50	0.83
24.	Wool gloves	1	2	1/2	4	2.0
25.	Wool sport cap	1	4	1/4	7	1.75
26.	Fur winter boots	1	3	1/3	40	13.3
27.	Shoes	1	2	1/2	20	10.0
28.	Walking shoes	1	2	1/2	30	15.0
29.	Rubber footwear	1	3	1/3	8	2.7
30.	Slippers	1	1	1	3	3.0
31.	Cotton blanket	1	9	1/9	16	1.8
32.	Pillow	1	7	1/7	1.40	1.34
33.	Flannelette blanket	1	7	1/7	10	1.43
34.	Blanket covers	2	4	2/4	10.10	5.05
35.	Sheets	2	4	2/4	5.10	2.55
36.	Pillow covers	3	4	3/4	1.90	1.43
37.	Personal towel	2	3	2/3	0.80	0.13
38.	Bath towel	2	4	2/4	3.80	1.9
39.	Kitchen towel	2	3	2/3	1.10	0.73
40.	Handkerchief	5	2	5/2	0.65	1.63
41.	Recreation footwear	1	1	1	25	25.0
42.	Summer footwear	1	2	1/2	9	4.5
43.	Sport suits	1	3	1/3	55	18.3
44.	Umbrella	1	5	1/5	18.50	3.7
45.	Gym shoes	1	3	1/3	4	1.3

TOTAL   per year   **409.5**
                per month   **34.13**

EXPENDITURES FOR BUYING DURABLE GOODS

	Amount Needed	Usage Period (in years)	Annual Purchase	Price in Rubles	Cost of Annual Purchase (Rubles)
Refrigerator	1	15	1/15	150	10.0
Washing machine	1	15	1/15	38	2.5
Electric lamps	10	1	10	0.20	2.0
Vacuum cleaner	1	12	1/12	25	2.0
Iron	1	7	1/7	7	1.0
Chandelier	1	10	1/10	23	2.3
Coffee grinder	1	10	1/10	23	2.3
Table lamp	1	10	1/10	8.50	0.8
Kitchen lamp	1	10	1/10	3.50	0.3
Electric razor	1	10	1/10	19	1.9
TV set (360x270)	1	12	1/12	200	16.7
Radio set	1	12	1/12	44	3.6
Tape recorder	1	10	1/10	150	15.0
Photo camera	1	12	1/12	32.50	2.7
Films	4	1	4	0.30	1.2
Cassettes (tape)	3	1	3	4.00	12.0
Alarm clock	1	10	1/10	4.50	0.0
Skis	1	6	1/6	13	2.0
Volleyball	1	4	1/4	7	1.0
Badminton racket	1	7	1/7	11	1.0
Skiing shoes	1	12	1/12	18.90	1.0
Bicycle	1	15	1/15	60	4.0
Chess	1	10	1/10	3.00	0.0
TOTAL per year					89.61
per month					7.47

dure for computing the minimum consumer budget of a male of employable age drawn up by the USSR State Committee for Labor in 1989.

Indexing minimum incomes (wages, pensions, student grants) to the conventionally computed value for the subsistence minimum will certainly ensure the expanded reproduction of poverty in the future.

The nature of manpower required to sustain the development of society — manpower geared to constant improvement — requires an entirely different approach to defining its cost. The problem is not in the value of the minimum consumer budget, but rather in its structure, which should be geared differently, for meeting both the physiological and cultural-intellectual requirements of the individual. This would mean transition to a different system of values, which cannot be effected in an evolutionary way in the USSR. The country needs a cardinal reform in the relations of distribution and new principles of forming incomes. Appropriate mechanisms should be incorporated into the government's policy of income-structuring.

CALCULATION OF EXPENDITURES FOR PURCHASING FURNITURE

	Amount Needed	Usage Period	Annual Purchase	Price in Rubles	Cost of Annual Purchase (Rubles)
LIVING ROOMS					
Wardrobe	1	20	1/20	187	9.35
Bookcase	1	20	1/20	180	9
Sideboard	1	20	1/20	250	12.5
Table	1	15	1/15	55	3.7
Sofa 1	1	5	1/15	250	16.7
Bed	1	20	1/20	120	6.0
Writing table	1	20	1/20	65	3.25
Chair	6	10	3/5	18	10.8
TV platform	1	15	1/15	46	3.06
Armchair	2	15	2/15	46	6.1
Ledge	1	10	1/10	2	0.2
KITCHEN					
Dining table	1	15	1/15	32	2.1
Cupboard	1	20	1/20	22	1.1
Stool	4	10	2/5	4.8	1.92
Kitchen table	1	15	1/15	56.0	3.73
Breadbasket	1	5	1/15	4	0.8
ANTEROOM					
Hall stand	1	20	1/20	123	6.15
Mirror	1	20	1/20	15	0.75
BATHROOM					
Mirror	1	20	1/20	5	0.25
Shelf	1	20	1/20	7	0.35
TOTAL per year					97.81
per month					8.15

CALCULATION OF EXPENDITURES FOR THE PURCHASE OF ITEMS OF ECONOMIC/HOUSEHOLD USE — UTENSILS

	Amount Needed	Usage Period	Annual Purchase	Price in Rubles	Cost of Annual Purchase (Rubles)
Dinnerware					
Soup plates	6	7	6/7	0.72	0.62
Dinner plates	6	7	6/7	0.66	0.57
Soup spoons	6	20	3/10	0.55	0.17
Table knives	6	20	3/10	1.55	0.35
Forks 6	20	3/10	0.55	0.17	
Tea Sets					
Tea kettle	1	6	1/6	1.45	0.24
Cups and saucers	6	6	1	1.15	1.15
Butter dish	1	6	1/6	1.05	0.18
Wine glasses	6	6	1	0.40	0.40
Teaspoons	6	20	3/10	0.40	0.12
Glasses	6	6	1	0.80	0.80
Fish dish	1	6	1/6	0.60	0.10
Sugar container	1	6	1/6	0.60	0.10
Kitchenware					
Aluminum pot	1	10	1/10	0.85	0.085
Enamel pot					
5 liter	1	10	1/10	4.95	0.495
2.5 liter	1	10	1/10	3.15	0.315
1.6 liter	1	10	1/10	1.75	0.175
Cast-iron frying pan	1	9	1/9	0.75	0.083
Enamel tea kettle	1	6	1/6	3.2	0.53
Container for milk	1	6	1/6	4.0	0.67
Aluminum sieve	1	8	1/8	2.0	0.25
Serving spoon	1	15	1/15	1.7	0.11
Kitchen knife	1	20	1/20	1.0	0.05
Meat grinder	1	15	1/15	5.0	0.35
Washtub	1	8	1/8	2.0	0.25
Enamel jug	1	6	1/6	0.65	0.108
Container for boiling cloths	1	7	1/7	6.6	0.94
Bucket	1	6	1/6	1.7	0.28
Roasting pan	1	15	1/15	2.7	0.18
Cutting board	2	5	2/1	50.4	0.16
TOTAL per year					10.0
per month					0.83

SYSTEM OF COEFFICIENTS AND DIFFERENTIALS IN THE BUDGETS OF THE MINIMUM STANDARD OF LIVING DISTRIBUTED ACCORDING TO SEX AND AGE GROUPS OF THE POPULATION

Sex and age groups of the population	Coefficients where 1 is set for a city man, age 30-59	
	City	Village
Children: boys		
0-2 yrs	0.3	0.3
3-6 yrs	0.4	0.3
7-12 yrs	0.5	0.4
13-17	0.7	0.5
Children: girls		
0-2 yrs	0.3	0.3
3-6 yrs	0.4	0.3
7-12 yrs	0.5	0.4
13-17 yrs	0.7	0.6
Men		
18-29 yrs	1.04	0.9
30-59 yrs	1.0	0.9
60 yrs & older	0.7	0.6
Women		
18-29 yrs	1.01	0.9
30-54 yrs	0.98	0.88
55 yrs & older	0.7	0.7
Married couples		
18-29 yrs	1.9	1.6
Family: parents 18-29 yrs, boy 7 yrs	2.4	2.0
Family: parents 18-29 boy 2 yrs girl 6 yrs	2.6	2.2
Family:parents 30-54 boy 4, girl 8, boy 14	3.5	2.9
Family:parents 30-54 girl 16 woman-pensioner	3.0	2.5
Single mother 18-29 child (boy 6)	1.4	1.2
Single mother 30-54 2 children (boy 6, girl 10)	1.9	1.6

ESTIMATION OF POSSIBLE SCALE OF PRIVATIZATION
(DATA ON THE BEGINNING OF 1989)

		Balance of property	Property share subject to privatization (%)	Property subject to privatization (billion rubles)
1.	Capital funds including cattle	2699	55.9	1509
1.1.	Capital production funds	1808		1011
1.1.1	in industry	883	56.0	574
1.1.2	in agriculture	354	65.0	230
1.1.3	in building	94	75.0	70
1.1.4	in transport and communication	378	15.0	57
1.1.5	in trade, restaurants, MTS, etc.	99	80.0	80
1.2	Capital non-productive funds	891	55.9	498
1.2.1	residential housing	499	80.0	400
1.2.2	communal and consumer services	123	80.0	98
2.	Unfinished construction	190-200*	30.0	60
3.	Material reserves	540-550*	50.0	270
4.	Sale of land			
TOTAL				1839

* Estimate on July 1, 1990

ESTIMATION OF POSSIBLE VOLUMES OF PRIVATIZATION IN TRADE

(DATA 1989)

---

1. SALES OF SMALL SHOPS

Trading area in Sq m	Quantity (thousands)	Number of employees in a shop	Cost of capital funds (million rubles)	Price Per 1 Shop (1000 rubles)
to 30	98.2	2	873	2-6
3-100	299.9	4	6554	9-16
100-250	127.9	11	8012	25-40
TOTAL	526.0	–	15439	–

when sold are				
100%	526.0		8000-12000	
50%	263.0		4000-6000	
25%	131.5		2000-4000	
10%	52.6		1000-2000	

2. PRIVATIZATIONS OF MEDIUM-SIZE SHOPS

250-650	57800	26-30	9600	120-160
650-1500	9800	55-70	3520	250-300

when sold are				
100%	57600		8000-10000	
50%	28800		4000-5000	
25%	14400		2000-3000	
10%	7700		1000-2000	

3. SHARES OF LARGE DEPARTMENT STORES

more than				
1500	1700	150-20	2134	800-1100

when sold are				
100%	1700		1100-1600	
50%	850		600-800	
25%	425		300-400	
10%	170		150-200	

TOTAL WITH DIFFERENT VARIANTS OF PRIVATIZATION

Variant		Total sales (billion rubles)	State revenue (billion rubles)
1.	50% small shops	4-6	2-3.
	10% medium-size shops	1-2	0.5-1
	10% large shops		
	TOTAL	5.2-8.2	2.6-4.2
2.	100% small shops 8-12	4-6	
	25% medium-size shops	2-3	1-2
	50% large shops 0.6-0.8	0.6-0.8	
	TOTAL	10.6-15.8	5.6-8.8
3.	100% small shops	8-12	4-6.
	50% medium-size shops	4-5	2-3.
	100% large shops	1-1.5	1-1.5
	TOTAL	13-18.5	7-10.5

PRINCIPLES FOR BALANCING THE UNION BUDGET IN FOURTH QUARTER OF 1990

Calculation basis — the plan of the budget for the fourth quarter of 1990 provided by the USSR Finance Ministry:

- income — 46.9 billion rubles
- expenses — 62.5 billion rubles
- deficit — 15.6 billion rubles.

1. Reduction of expenses:
   a) Direct reduction:
      of capital investments — 20 percent;
      of operative expenses — 30 to 50 percent;
      of military expenses (buying military equipment) — 50 to 70 percent;
      of foreign trade expenses (freezing the assistance and credits to other countries at a zero level for a quarter);
   b) Fixing protected items:
      social and cultural programs;
      police expenditures;
      State debt servicing expenditures;
      election expenditures;
   c) Reduction of all unprotected contracts by 10 to 15 percent;
      As a result: reduction of Union budget expenses by 10 billion rubles.
2. Income increase:
   reorientation of foreign trade stimulating export production by 10 to 20 percent, or 1.5–3.0 billion rubles;
   increase of production of tax-consuming commodities;
   growth of circulation tax by 10 to 20 percent, or 0.8-1.5 billion rubles.

Result: income growth by 2-4 billion rubles
   Possible reduction of Union budget deficit to 1.6-3.6 billion rubles.

CALCULATIONS FOR FORECASTING

Table 1
INCOMES AND EXPENDITURES

		billion rubles	
	1989	1990 (forecast)	
		VERSION 1	VERSION 2
INCOMES			
1. Wages and salaries	408.5	455	455
2. Pensions, grants, scholarships	76.8	87	87
3. Interest	8	9	12
4. Other	64	74	74
TOTAL	557.3	625	628
EXPENDITURES			
1. Goods and services	403.4	490	490
2. Obligatory & voluntary payments	63.8	72	72
3. Hard currency and precious metals	1	2	15
4. Purchase of housing, land, garages	-	-	5
5. Savings + money-supply increase	62.1	61	46
TOTAL	557.3	625	628
SAVINGS			
1. Bank accounts	337.9	367	361
2. Cash	105.1	124	110
3. Certificates	2.8	4	4
4. Other	43.3	56	55
MATERIAL ASSETS			
1. Individual property	860	940	970
2. Land & housing	160	166	176

Extraordinary measures of the monetary policies will be bound to have the most positive effect on decreasing state budget deficit. Table 2 also shows 2 versions of 1990 budget.

Decreasing spending in all nonsocial (unprotected) areas by 5 percent of annual volume or 20 percent of spending in the fourth quarter (as the program

Table 2
INCOME AND EXPENSE IN THE STATE BUDGET
(BILLION RUBLES)

		1990 forecast			
		VERSION 1		VERSION 2	
	1989	year	quarter	year	quarter
INCOME					
1. Commercial income	111.1	121.9	30.5	122	30.5
2. Profit levies	115.5	121.6	30.4	120	30
3. Social insurance	33.1	44.8	11.2	45	11.3
4. Foreign business activities	67.2	59.6	14.9	60	15
5. Taxes from population	41.7	43.5	10.9	43.5	10.0
6. Others	33.3	38.5	9.6	38.5	9.6
TOTAL INCOME	401.9	429.9	107.5	430	107.3
EXPENDITURES					
1. Financing national economy including:	200.1	188.2	47.1	175	34.3
Capital investment	68.0	42.2	10.6	40.0	8.8
Subsidies	1.8	16.8	4.2	12.6	0
Day-to-day spending	8.0	11.8	3.0	11.2	2.4
Food subsidies	97.9	95.9	24.0	91.2	19.3
Others	24.4	21.5	5.3	20.0	3.3
2. Financing foreign business activities	28.4	26.9	6.7	25.6	5.4
3. Financing social and cultural events	139.3	160.5	40.1	160.5	40.1
4. Research	10.1	10.9	2.7	10.0	2.5
5. Defense	75.2	71.0	17.8	67.5	14.3
6. Others	29.9	32.4	8.1	31.0	6.7
TOTAL SPENDING	482.6	489.9	122.5	469.6	103.3
DEFICIT	-80.7	-60.0	-15	-39.6	+4.

begins on October 1). Subsidies to unprofitable enterprises are practically discontinued. This will bring them to the brink of bankruptcy and force them to change prices for goods they manufacture and issue debt or privatize.

The forecast for income and expense in industries is shown in Table 3. In conditions of severe limitations on budget spending the subsidy income of enterprises is decreased, capital investments of enterprises and organizations will be the first to be cut back.

Table 3
INCOME AND EXPENSE OF ENTERPRISES AND ORGANIZATIONS
(Including Collective Farms) (billion rubles)

		1990 forecast	
	1989	VERSION 1	VERSION 2
INCOME			
1. Profit	270	265	253
2. Amortization	141	146	146
TOTAL	411	411	399
EXPENSE			
1. Payments to budget	117	123.3	121.3
2. Repairs	63	67	67
3. Financing capital investment	144	143.5	135.7
4. Bonuses, social and other spendings	87	77.2	75

The State budget deficit will decrease by 25 billion rubles by the end of the year, accounting for 2.5 percent of the GKP. Funds incoming into the state budget are 4 billion rubles higher than outgoing funds in the fourth quarter. Restrictive monetary policies will lead to decreases of available cash and lower liquidity. The state of the money supply is shown in Table 4.

Table 4
MONEY SUPPLY
(billion rubles)*

		12/31/1990	
	12/31/89	VERSION 1	VERSION 2
M$_0$: available cash (held by the population and enterprises)	110	130	116
M$_1$: M$_0$ plus savings in banks, bonds, insurance	357	407	360
M$_3$: M$_1$ plus	704	758	734
short-term accounts	136	158	191
self-accounting enterprises' funds	108	110	100
funds of budget and public organizations State Insurance	103	83	83

* Without foreign operations

Table 5
MEASURES TO DECREASE THE STATE BUDGET AND THE MONEY SUPPLY

	100 days 1990	Jan.- March 1991	Apr.- June 1991	July- Sept. 1991	Oct.- Dec. 1991	1991
Decreasing budget deficit						
Cuts in capital investment	2.2	2.2	2.2	2.2	2.2	8.8
Cuts of subsidies	9	8	8	8	8	32
Cuts in financing foreign business activities	1.3	1.3	1.3	1.3	1.3	5.2
Cuts in defense spending	3.5	3.5	3.5	3.5	3.5	14
Cuts of other spending	3.5	3.5	3.5	3.5	3.5	14
Cuts of deficit by pricing	-	5	7	7	7	26
TOTAL	**19.5**	**23.5**	**25.5**	**25.5**	**25.5**	**100**
Decreasing liquidity (in current prices)						
Sales of hard currency	10	10	8	3	3	24
Sales of gold	2	5	2	-	-	7
Sales of apartments, land, garages	5	10	10	7	7	34
Sales of Reform loan bonds	1	4	4	3	3	14
Sales of unfinished construction projects	1	5	5	3	1	14
Privatization of small firms	0.5	1	1	3	10	15
Sales of stock	0.5	1	1	3	10	15
TOTAL	**20**	**36**	**31**	**22**	**34**	**123**

One of the major results of restrictive monetarist policies will be that the M_1 liquidity component will go down from 407 billion rubles to 360 billion. Funds in accounts of enterprises will be decreased mostly because loans will be more difficult to obtain.

Growth of prices for products for industries will be determined by new tariffs for insurance (38 percent), and the need to raise prices for fuel and power. When the latter rise twofold initially (30 to 40 percent more later) wholesale price growth will amount to 25 to 30 percent in the first 3 months. Protection of consumer goods prices will be provided for by redistribution of taxes on turnover from processing industries to the prices on goods in the middle of the chain and rent in raw materials industries, as well as decreasing prices in processing industries. Table 8 shows 3 versions of price indices.

Table 6
BALANCE OF INCOME AND EXPENSE FOR THE POPULATION

	VERSION 1					VERSION 2					VERSION 3				
	1 qtr*	2 qtr	3 qtr	4 qtr	1991	1 qtr	2 qtr	3 qtr	4 qtr	1991	1 qtr	2 qtr	3 qtr	4 qtr	1991
INCOME															
1. Wages	123	144	150	160	577	123	144	150	160	577	123	144	159	169	595
2. Scholarships, grants, and pensions	25	30	31	34	120	25	30	31	34	120	25	30	35	3	128
3. Interest	7	7	8	9	31	7	7	8	9	31	7	10	12	14	43
4. Other	28	30	30	30	118	28	30	30	30	118	28	32	35	37	132
Total	183	211	219	233	846	183	211	219	23	846	183	216	241	258	898
EXPENSE															
1. Goods and services	133	156	173	183	638	158	178	173	18	692	158	191	213	22	790
2. Obligatory and voluntary payments	20	23	24	26	93	20	23	24	26	93	20	25	28	30	103
3. Hard-currency, precious metals	15	10	3	3	31	2	2	3	3	10	5	0	0	0	5
4. Housing, land, etc.	15	15	10	10	60	3	4	10	10	27	0	0	0	0	0
5. Savings and increase in money supply	0	4	9	11	24	0	4	9	11	24	0	0	0	0	0
TOTAL	183	211	219	233	846	183	211	219	233	846	183	216	241	258	898
Price increases (%)	112	119	109	105	153	130	113	100	105	155	132	121	111	107	190
SAVINGS															
1. Bank accounts	361	365	373	384	384	400	404	413	424	424	422	455	440	430	430
2. Cash	110	110	110	110	110	110	110	110	110	110	110	130	145	155	155
3. Other	60	60	60	60	60	60	60	60	60	60	60	60	60	60	60

*qtr 1 - January-March, qtr 2 - April-June, qtr 3 - July-September, qtr 4 - October-December.

Budget income and spending is shown in Table 9. It is clear from the table that after emergency measures are carried out and when pricing factors begin to operate income will go up by 146 billion rubles (206 billion in version 3), but indexing budget spending and new spending such as unemployment benefits as well as great increase of interest paid to service state debt will

Table 7
PRICE INDICES
(Consumer Goods)

	Jan.-March	April-June	July-Sept.	October-December	1991
1. FOOD					
1	1.25	1.25	1.0	1.0	1.56
2	1.41	1.17	1.0	1.0	1.65
3	1.41	1.18	1.08	1.06	1.76
2. LIQUOR					
1	1.0	1.1	1.08	1.0	1.18
2	1.32	1.03	1.0	1.0	1.36
3	1.32	1.12	1.04	1.03	1.58
3. LIGHT INDUSTRY GOODS					
1	1.0	1.13	1.08	1.05	1.22
2	1.28	1.06	1.0	1.05	1.36
3	1.28	1.13	1.06	1.04	1.59
4. OTHER GOODS AND SERVICES					
1	1.0	1.18	1.16	1.11	1.52
2	1.28	1.16	1.0	1.11	1.65
3	1.28	1.3	1.186	1.11	2.14
TOTAL					
1	1.12	1.19	1.09	1.05	1.53
2	1.3	1.13	1.0	1.05	1.55
3	1.32	1.21	1.11	1.07	1.9

Table 8
WHOLESALE PRICE INDICES

	VERSION 1	VERSION 2	VERSION 3
Metallurgy	1.6	1.6	1.7
Fuel and power	2.18	2.18	1.7
Machine building	1.12	1.12	1.25
Chemistry & timber	1.24	1.24	1.36
Construction materials	1.3	1.3	1.45
Timber	1.2	1.35	1.6
Food	1.56	1.65	1.76
Agriculture	1.12	1.15	1.33
Construction	1.12	1.12	1.25
Communications & transport	1.4	1.4	1.5
Trade, others	1.3	1.3	1.44
TOTAL	**1.3**	**1.3**	**1.45**

Table 9
1991 STATE BUDGET—INCOME AND EXPENSE

	VERSION 1					VERSION 2					VERSION 3				
	1 qtr*	2 qtr	3 qtr	4 qtr	1991	1 qtr	2 qtr	3 qtr	4 qt	1991	1 qtr	2 qtr	3 qtr	4 qtr	1991
INCOME															
1. Turnover tax	34	38	39	39	150	36	40	40	40	156	36	43	48	50	177
2. Income tax	20	20	20	20	80	20	20	20	20	80	25	25	25	25	100
3. Rent 15	15	15	15	60	15	15	15	15	60	20	20	20	20		80
4. Insurance	38	43	43	46	170	38	43	43	46	170	38	43	43	46	170
5. Foreign business activitiies	15	15	15	15	60	15	15	15	15	60	15	15	15	15	60
6. Personal tax	11	13	13	13	50	11	13	13	13	50	11	13	13	13	50
7. Other income															
TOTAL	143	154	155	158	610	145	156	156	159	616	155	169	174	179	677
EXPENSE															
1. Financing national economy	37	37	38	38	150	37	37	38	38	150	40	42	44	44	170
2. Social and cultural	51	56	58	61	226	51	56	58	61	226	54	59	64	67	244
3. Unemployment benefits	2	4	6	8	20	2	4	6	8	20	3	5	7	10	25
4. Defense	20	20	20	20	80	20	20	20	20	80	23	23	22	22	90
5. Foreign business activities	10	10	10	10	40	10	10	10	10	40	10	10	10	10	40
6. Internal dDebt service	10	10	10	10	40	10	10	10	10	40	10	10	10	10	40
7. Other	14	14	14	14	56	14	14	14	14	56	15	15	15	15	60
TOTAL	144	151	156	161	612	144	151	156	161	612	159	168	176	182	685
Net	-1	+3	-1	-3	-2	+1	+5	0	-2	+4	+1	-4	-2	-3	-8

*qtr 1 - January-March, qtr 2 - April-June, qtr 3 - July-September, qtr 4 - October-December.

bring up spending by 120 billion rubles (183 billion). However, a package of strict financial measures will ensure that there is no deficit in 1991.

The profit of enterprises after taxes are paid (80-100 billion rubles) will be used to pay bonuses and for other social purposes. With 10 to 25 percent interest rates enterprises will have to pay 30-80 billion rubles to service debts. Transformation of enterprises into joint stock societies will bring another 10-15 billion into the state budget and will be used to pay interest on state debt and/or indexing people's bank accounts (versions 2,3).

Table 10
MONEY SUPPLY DYNAMICS IN 1991
(billion rubles)
(VERSIONS 1 AND 2)

	01.01. 1991	04.01 1991	07.01 1991	10.01 1991	01.01 1992
M0: cash held by people and enterprises	116	116	116	116	116
M1: M0 plus savings in long term accounts, bonds, securities, insurance	360	360	360	360	360
M3: M1 plus short term accounts	734	734/773	738/777	746/786	767/727
funds of enterprises, organizations, other	191	191/230*	195/234	203/243	214/254

* Version 1 - accounts not indexed
Version 2 - accounts indexed

Accounts are indexed in the case of sharp growth of prices by 40 billion rubles that has to be compensated by a sharp increase of interest rates (in the case of price growth), payment of interest on state debt and profits from privatization (if they reach sufficient level).

In the case of a sharp increase of prices (version 3), the population's accounts will be indexed twice for the sums of 61 billion rubles and 53 billion rubles. More cash may be needed to ensure enough for circulation. It can be obtained by decreasing demand accounts.

Table 11
MONEY SUPPLY IN 1991
(billion rubles)
(VERSION 3)

	01.01 1991	01.04 1991	01.07 1991	01.10 1991	01.01 1992
M0:	116	116	136	150	160
M1:	1360	360	360	360	360
M3:	3734	795	848	848	848
including: short term accounts	191	252	305	305	305
accounts of enterprises and organizations	183	183	183	183	183

INDEX

DATE DUE